T0244749

Reading Kierkegaard Devotionally

From the same author

Kierkegaard's Metaphors

*Toward the Final Crossroads: A Festschrift for Edna &
Howard Hong* (editor)

*Sober Cannibals, Drunken Christians: Melville,
Kierkegaard, & Tragic Optimism in Polarized
Worlds*

*Becoming Human: Kierkegaardian Reflections on
Ethical Models in Literature*

Taking Kierkegaard Personally: First Person Responses
(co-editor)

Reading Kierkegaard Devotionally

Jamie Lorentzen

MERCER UNIVERSITY PRESS
Macon, Georgia

MUP/ P704

© 2024 by Mercer University Press
Published by Mercer University Press
1501 Mercer University Drive
Macon, Georgia 31207

28 27 26 25 24   5 4 3 2 1

Books published by Mercer University Press are
printed on acid-free paper that meets the
requirements of the American National Standard
for Information Sciences—Permanence of Paper
for Printed Library Materials.

Printed and bound in the United States.

This book is set in Adobe Garamond.

Cover/jacket design by Burt&Burt.

ISBN   978-0-88146-955-4
Cataloging-in-Publication Data is available from
the Library of Congress

Contents

MERCER UNIVERSITY PRESS

Endowed by

TOM WATSON BROWN
and
THE WATSON-BROWN FOUNDATION, INC.

In memory of Edna Hatlestad Hong
(1913-2007)

There is not one single living human being who does not despair a little, who does not secretly harbor an unrest, an inner strife, a disharmony, an anxiety about an unknown something or a something he does not even dare to try to know, an anxiety about some possibility in existence or an anxiety about himself…, a sickness of the spirit that signals its presence at rare intervals in and through an anxiety he cannot explain.

—Søren Kierkegaard's *Anti-Climacus*

[Let] a person with a deeply religious need…suddenly come upon one of the old devotional books and there quite rightly find spiritual trial described—indeed, he would very likely be as happy as Robinson Crusoe was to meet Friday.

—Søren Kierkegaard's *Johannes Climacus*

1

Preliminary Note.
Kierkegaard as a Devotional
Writer and Reader

Danish writer Søren Kierkegaard (1813-1855) penned three authorships: an esthetically oriented pseudonymous authorship, a religiously oriented signed authorship, and a personal authorship comprised of journals, papers, and notebooks. In the following pages, I identify Kierkegaard's religious authorship as well as thousands of religiously oriented entries in his personal authorship under the genre of devotional literature, which I define as literature that recalls the reader to sacred text in ways that call the reader to respond ethically to that text.

As for the more popular esthetically oriented pseudonymous books: Kierkegaard saw them as prompts to his reader (whom he presumes to be nominally acquainted with sacred text) to reread sacred text, to "once again to read through solo, if possible in a more inward way, the original text of individual human existence-relationships, the old familiar text handed down from the fathers." This assertion is located at the end of the five-page "First and Last Explanation" that he added at the last minute to the end of his book, *Concluding Unscientific Postscript*—the book Kierkegaard thought at the time would terminate his pseudonymous authorship. Comporting with George Pattison's claim that "there is no final gap between the pseudonymous writings and the signed religious works," this little "postscript" that Kierkegaard adds to the end of his big *Postscript* bridges whatever gap any reader may perceive to be between the two authorships, thereby suggesting that the whole of the pseudonymous authorship may also be (albeit loosely) categorized under the genre of devotional literature.

Virtually all of Kierkegaard's works, in other words, invite the reader to read and reread scriptural text before responding along the lines that Pattison considers when he writes about seeking in Kierkegaard's texts a "relationship between a model of devotional reading in which the individual is concerned with his self-development and the summons to step out onto the public stage of active witness."

In his 1848 intellectual autobiography *The Point of View for my Work as an Author*, Kierkegaard maintains that the pseudonymous authorship in general and his *Concluding Unscientific Postscript* in particular are not "strictly speaking... religious." Another passage from *The Point of View* nevertheless shows Kierkegaard continuing to explain, prompt, and remind the reader always to carry forward any direct or indirect religious tailings and underpinnings that are evoked by his pseudonyms (in this passage, *carrying forward* equates to forwarding a number in an arithmetic calculation to the next column):

> But above all do not forget one thing, the number carried that you have, that it is the religious that you are to have to come forward. Or, if you are able to do so, portray the esthetic with all its bewitching charm, if possible captivate the other person, portray it with the kind of passionateness whereby it particularly appeals to him, hilariously to the hilarious, sadly to the sad, wittily to the witty, etc.—but above all do not forget one thing, the number carried that you have, that it is the religious that is to come forward. Just do it; do not fear to do it, for truly it can be done only in much fear and trembling.

Here and everywhere, Kierkegaard meets especially his secular and critical readers at whatever stages they are along life's way, which suggests why he wrote so many pages entertaining so many secular and esthetically oriented ideas. "My entire existence," Kierkegaard writes that same year in a journal entry, "is an epigram for the sake of awakening"—and by "awakening," Kierkegaard ultimately means an awakening to the religious (what his Anti-Climacus calls "an awareness of the holy") both for himself and for his reader.

Even in texts filled with exquisite negative role models, irony, and lyricism—from, for example, pseudonym A's "Diapsalmata" and "The Immediate Erotic Stages" to "The Seducer's Diary" in *Either/Or* I—*carrying forward* Kierkegaard's religious presuppositions attunes readers' ears to hear the call of the ethical and ethical-religious as distant but distinct antiphons resonating above and before the alluring din. Such flights of Kierkegaard's fancy were crafted to help readers imagine deeper layers of reflection and calling wherein the essence of devotional reading resides, those layers that are meant to prompt inward reception and positive ethical response beyond personal admiration for or critical literary-philo-sophical-academic responses to the texts.

The "religious that is to come forward" *on the part of the reader* ultimately becomes the fruit by which Kierkegaard wants his literary tree to be known, the fruit being not Kierkegaard's literary works—they are merely the blossoms—but instead the reader's own inward and actively upward existential work. A few of Kierkegaard's larger literary blossoms issued from the pseudonymous branch of that tree include the Jylland preacher's sermon at the end of *Either/Or* II, Vigilius Haufniensis's final chapter in *The Concept of Anxiety*, Anti-Climacus's final chapter in *The Sickness unto Death*, and H. H.'s *Two Ethical-Religious Essays*. In addition, as Christopher Barnett maintains in his book *Kierkegaard,*

6

Pietism, and Holiness, a "religious undercurrent" in Kierkegaard's esthetic works is suggested by the religiously "monastic overtones" of many of his pseudonyms, including Johannes Climacus and Anti-Climacus (namesakes of Middle Eastern monk John Climacus [579-649]), Frater Taciturnus ("Silent Brother"), Hilarius Bookbinder ("probably," according to Barnett, named "after the fourth-century patristic theologian, Hilary"), Johannes de Silentio ("John the Silent"), and Victor Eremita ("Victorious Hermit").

The heart of Kierkegaard's canon, however, remains his signed authorship, that patently religiously oriented oeuvre composed primarily of discourses in which his preferred descriptor *det opbyggelige* is generally translated into English as either "the edifying" or "the upbuilding." (*The Gyldendal Danish/English Dictionary* definitions for variants of *det opbyggelige* include *opbygge* (vb.)—build (up), construct, edify; *opbyggelig* (adj.)—edifying, devotional; and *opbyggelsesskrift* (n.)—devotional book.) The Hongs translate the adjective *opbyggelig* as "upbuilding" instead of "edifying" or "devotional," noting that "upbuilding" evokes a wider range of meanings both etymologically and metaphorically than does "edifying" and "devotional."

As much as the Hongs' detailed and multi-layered defense of the word "upbuilding" is compelling, and as much as I respect why translators before and after the Hongs (including Walter Lowrie and David Swenson before them, and Bruce Kirmmse and his co-translators after them) side with the more morally charged "edifying" and "edification," I raise a small flag here for the narrowest and most limiting descriptor, "devotional." For there is something about so much of Kierkegaard's authorship that evokes the fundamental nature of devotional literature. Such a descriptor is commensurate with what the Hongs mean when they write that "for Kierkegaard 'the up-building' (*det opbyggelige*) means everything that contributes to interiorization or inward deepening, that is, the individual's appropriation of ethical and religious truths." And even though the adjective *devotional* (more than "edifying" and especially "up-building") is a word that, like *obedience*, sticks in the throats of many modern and secular readers, its noun variant is "a devotional," that is, a meditation that takes place outside of Sunday morning church services. My point here is that the element of authority—more specifically, the element of being *without* authority—that is attached to the word "devotional" is not unlike Kierkegaard's insistence that his religious discourses are not sermons because he was never a pastor. Such writings are without ecclesiastical authority and so assume the rank of devotionals. It is possible, then, to hold conference with God not only in a church but in a living room or kitchen or park or wherever one chooses to practice devotion.

—I thank Rev. Donald Fox for bringing this notion of authority to my attention after he remembered a 1925 church record book that his Lower Coon Valley Norwegian Lutheran Church in Stoddard, Wisconsin still uses; there is a place in that book to record *opbygelser*—that is, *devotional services* that took place without a pastor.

ભ

Evidence of Kierkegaard's own devotional life also speaks to how his habit of reading devotional literature begot the writing of his own devotional literature. Barnett notes that Kierkegaard was a great collector and reader of classic devotional literature (known in German scholarship under the genre *Erbauungsliteratur* [edifying or upbuilding literature]) and that his library was well stocked with devotional works by Bernard of Clairvaux (1090-1153), Johannes Tauler (1300-61), Thomas à Kempis (1380-1471), Johann Arndt (1555-1621), Christian Scriver (1629-93), Philipp Jacob Spener (1635-1705), August Hermann Franke (1663-1727), Jans Adolph Brorson (1694-1764), and Gerhard Terstegen (1697-1769). Barnett also writes that "by way of the Moravian Brethren—understood here both in terms of his family and in terms of Copenhagen's *Brødresocietet* [Society of Brothers]—Kierkegaard encountered upbuilding writings from a young age and maintained an affinity for them throughout his life." The literature, read alone or in small groups, was a means by which believers could participate "in church *outside* church—a way of making ordinary life holy, of 'upbuilding' the everyday." Barnett also notes that Kierkegaard had written in one journal entry that he "is reading Tauler for his own 'edification' [*Opbyggelse*]," what Barnett adds as being "one of the highest compliments he pays to an author signifying that, opposite Tauler, a posture of earnestness is appropriate," for it "nurtures piety and so is propaedeutic to ethico-religious development." Just as Kierkegaard always hoped to find the religiously oriented reader whom he often affectionately calls "*my* reader," devotional author Johannes Tauler may be said to have found *his* reader in Søren Kierkegaard here. Meanwhile, Kierkegaard notes in the same journal entry that he discovered a "striking similarity" between what Tauler had written in his *Nachfolgung des armen Lebens Jesu Christi* [*Meditations on the Life and Passion of Our Lord Jesus Christ*] and what Kierkegaard himself had written in his *Christian Discourses.*

In addition to Barnett's assessment, Kierkegaard scholar Perry LeFevre maintains that Kierkegaard devoted a definite time every day "regularly and with monastic precision" to the reading of devotional books. Furthermore, Kierkegaard biographer Clare Carlisle offers a specific account of the fruits of Kierkegaard's 1844 devotional reading. It is an account in which Johann Arndt's *True Christianity* informs some of Kierkegaard's own devotional writings in such a way that Kierkegaard's *Four Upbuilding Discourses* (1844)

> echoed Arndt's *True Christianity* in their emphasis on suffering and human frailty. Arndt insisted that "without misery God does not appear to man, and without the knowledge of misery man does not find God's grace." In his discourse "To Need God is a Human Being's Highest Perfection," Kierkegaard acknowledged that a deep spiritual need "makes life more difficult," but explained that a person becomes conscious of God through the "piecemeal experience" of his own anxiety, confusion, despair—and "in this difficulty his life also acquires ever deeper and deeper meaning." …Reading Arndt clarified and deepened Kierkegaard's conviction already expressed in *Fear and Trembling*: that joy lies on the far side of suffering, that struggle must precede consolation, that "only the one who was in anxiety finds rest."

⚥

Modelled after devotional writing practices of yore, the reflective rigor and religious inwardness to which Kierkegaard aspired as a devotional reader and prompted as a devotional writer were meant to maximize and concentrate time spent in reading and self-examination for the sake of responding daily to sacred text in ways that reflect what the reader understands to be true. Such rigor and inwardness were lacking in Golden Age Denmark (ca. 1800-50) in great part because of burgeoning fledgling newspaper presses and its feuilletons broadcasting daily news, gossip, light literature, criticism, and book reviews, which collectively co-opted readers' time each day from time that might otherwise have been spent tending to deeper layers of existence and reflection. (In one journal entry, Kierkegaard asks, "really, how many in Denmark have the time, the ability, and the interest to read?"—a question all the more salient worldwide as the age of the feuilleton of the nineteenth century transmogrified into newspaper, television, digital, and social media ages of the twentieth and twenty-first centuries.)*

Kierkegaard's own critique of the devolution of reading and writing habits in contemporary Danish culture is on full display in pseudonym Nicolaus Notabene's 1844 work, *Prefaces: Light Reading for People in Various Estates According to Time and*

---

*For a plenary discussion of Danish culture and especially its mass-marketing daily print culture in Kierkegaard's Copenhagen, see George Pattison's *Kierkegaard, Religion and the Nineteenth-Century Crisis of Culture* (Cambridge, United Kingdom: Cambridge University Press, 2002), especially pages 25-50.

Opportunity—both title and subtitle themselves being satiric salvos against the more modern reading initiatives that were increasingly accommodating, assuaging, and appeasing a more secularized and distracted reading public. In a three-page satiric glance at nineteenth-century Danish efforts to produce secularized devotional literature that constitutes the sixth "preface," Kierkegaard indirectly makes distinctions between what he considers to be watered-down devotional literature and rigorous devotional literature. And although Kierkegaard pays deference to Denmark's Bishop Jacob Peter Mynster, whom he acknowledges as contributing to Denmark's contemporary devotional literature, the seeds of Kierkegaard's eventual separation from Mynster's socio-religious brand of Golden Age state-managed Danish Christianity and accompanying devotional literature is evident. Kierkegaard scholar Bruce Kirmmse notes the "gulf" that increasingly yawns between Kierkegaard and Mynster beyond 1844, namely, "SK's continuing insistence that we make a humbling 'admission' of the inadequacy of our 'Christianity' in comparison with that of the saints and martyrs of the early Church. We ought, SK insists, to set aside a time each day to contemplate our imperfection in comparison with the greatness of those who dared all for faith, and we ought to contemplate the unfairness in the fact that we should all inherit the same salvation [that the saints and martyrs inherited...].

SK says that *this* sort of contemplation…emphasizes the importance of works and prepares one for the proper reception of grace…and this is very far indeed from Mynster's Christianity."

According to Kierkegaard, only by devotional practice that recollects backward to the saintly, martyred, sanctified lives of past exemplars may a reader begin to live life forward with the prospect of meeting the kinds of spiritual trials that make up the exemplary lives of the saints; by, as Kierkegaard writes, "tak[ing] the time to recall those glorious ones every single day"—that is, by reading them devotionally and regularly—"you have immediately at hand an example of a movement that is restlessness oriented toward inward deepening"—a restlessness that Kierkegaard equates with faith.

◌

Finally, two substantive obstacles to reading Kierkegaard devotionally should be introduced as elephants in the room, obstacles that will be further discussed throughout the remainder of this book.

Elephant in the Room #1 (especially for the religiously oriented reader): Despite being a devotional writer, Kierkegaard is neither apostle nor saint. He is also not one whose every word inspires obedience. Subsequently, he is not exempt from any reader's healthy skepticism and objectivity. Like anyone, there are logs in Kierkegaard's human eyes indicative of political blind spots and cultural prejudices, including unprovoked outbursts ranging from misogyny to unneighborly infighting with fellow Copenhageners to anti-Semitic utterances. Such outbursts are ones that Kierkegaard translator Bruce Kirmmse once described to me as akin to eating barbed wire. In addition, Kirmmse would most likely agree with Clare Carlisle when she writes that Kierkegaard "was a difficult person." Given Kirmmse's devotion to translating Kierkegaard's works, however, he also would probably agree with Carlisle when she adds that Kierkegaard was nevertheless "inspirational in his willingness to bear witness to the human condition." Such witnessing, which includes Kierkegaard himself suffering lapses in moral judgment, helps make many of his writings inviting as devotional literature; he ethically communicates to his reader a sense of intimate awareness and capability of being human and of needing neighbor love in ways that inspire devotional reception and actual response by both devotional writer and reader alike.

Elephant in the Room #2 (especially for the secularly oriented reader): The etymology of *devotion* (from Latin *devotio(n-)* from *devovere* "consecrate" or dedicate to a religious or divine purpose) speaks to Kierkegaard's religious presuppositions, which undergird and permeate not only Kierkegaard's most salient devotional works but the whole of his authorship. As Kierkegaard scholar Gregor Malantschuk notes, hundreds of references to God and of needing God exist from Kierkegaard's earliest works to his latest. Meanwhile, Kierkegaard himself claims that "from the very beginning" of his authorship and "in unconditional obedience" he has "basically lived like a scribe in [God's] office," and that Kierkegaard's self-proclaimed "work assignment" is "not the work of the poet passion or of the thinker passion, but of devotion to God." —It may be difficult, then, for any reader to imagine the kind of reading that Kierkegaard claims is required to be called *his* reader without the reader at least offering deference toward the central category of the religious in Kierkegaard's writings. What is at issue here is not that a reader needs to *believe* Kierkegaard's understanding of or belief in Christianity. Rather, a reader need only *understand* how Kierkegaard's understanding of and belief in a Christian Lutheran lexicon informs Kierkegaard's thought. It is only by such understanding that the reader may begin to appreciate the remarkable dialectical torque of Kierkegaard's thought, one that hews the cornerstone of his uniquely devotional literary edifice.

2

Testimonials from Contemporaries of Kierkegaard

May 21, 1851.... I dare, in spite of your strict injunction against it, to set pen to paper to thank you...for that infinitude of wealth I owe to you. Please do not think that I shall be guilty of the gross misunderstanding of becoming mired in personal adulation..., but you *must* allow a frail being a moment's pause.... [for] you do nothing *but put one in the right spot, focus the eye, expand the circle of vision, enchant the soul* with your mastery of language and thought—and that what you proclaim is not really a new discovery you have made but something that has endured as have eternal truths since—since eternity, of course. But in spite of this, inasmuch as nobody has proclaimed those truths to me before you did so in such a way that I could hear them, that is, with the ears of my soul so that they dwelt with me and became my eternal possessions.... From the very outset when you began to publish your pseudonymous works, I mean, from the time when you began that work of love of sharing your divine inspiration with mankind, *I* have pricked up my ears and listened lest I should miss any sound, even the faintest, of these magnificent harmonies, for everything resounded in my heart. This was what needed to be said—here I found answers to all my questions; nothing was omitted of that which interested me most profoundly—I was happy, reposing in blessed communion with this spirit which knew so well how to express everything I hardly knew I felt, much less thought, yet which had indeed been inside, though vague and confused…. I am never lonely, even when I am by myself for long periods of time, provided only that I have the company of these books, for they are, of all books, those that most closely resemble the company of a living person…. Please believe that again and again I have been roused by them to see myself more clearly and to understand my duty, to feel myself more closely tied to "the truth, the way, and the life."…Please believe as well that I have been struck with terror by those supreme demands of the ideal which you know how to throw into such sharp relief—and my distance from them!… But you are perfectly aware that you speak to a lethargic generation…. I sign myself with gladness and gratitude

One of your most devoted female readers, S. F.

☙

May 21, 1851. Dear Magister.... In the frivolous, or perhaps, as you remark somewhere, the melancholy spirit of the times, I long ignored God and my relation to him, but this was an unhappy state of affairs, as I soon realized. I sought comfort in prayer, but I felt that God would not hear me; I went to church, but my scattered thoughts would not follow those of the preacher; I tried, in the philosophy books that I could understand, to find rest for my lost soul, and I found some. I had read *Either/Or* with profound admiration, and I tried to obtain some of your works by borrowing since I could not afford to buy them. I received the *Christian Discourses* of 1848, which were not what I had wanted, but I read them—and how can I ever thank you enough? In them I found the source of life that has not failed me since. When I was troubled, I sought refuge there and found comfort; when need or chance brought me to church and I walked away downcast, conscious of one more sin for having been in the House of the Lord without reverence and humility, then I would read your discourses and find comfort. In everything that happened to me, in sorrow or in joy, this small portion of the riches you have bequeathed to the world became the constant source from which I drew comfort and sustenance.... I am a woman and dare only approach you under an assumed name.

With the deepest respect and gratitude,

e——e.

CR

March 19, 1852.... My soul is filled with gratitude for your having led me to self-understanding, thus bringing more peace and less sadness to my heart.... It is not to the clever Dr. Kjerkegaard that this is written, but to him who seems to me to comprehend all the inwardness of Christianity and who because of this inwardness will understand the feeling and need that made me, *contrary to my custom*, go so much outside myself that I *had to say thank you*; ...my consolation will have to be that I have only expressed myself to one soul and that only two eyes will light on this, eyes that look deeply enough into the human heart to be indulgent. This is not the enthusiastic thanks of an eighteen-year-old girl, but the abundant, profound thanks of a thirty-four-year-old unmarried woman who stands alone among strangers but who has gained clearer awareness of her innermost being through you—and thereby more peace and more courage not to let herself be overwhelmed by feelings which cannot be the truth for her, more strength to fight the good fight with constancy.

Yours gratefully, L. H.

CR

July 12, 1851…. Doctor S. Kierkegaard,…. Thank you, good doctor, for every shaft of light with which you enlighten the dark lives of your fellow man, "dark," I suppose, because the eyes are not truly open.

Your sincerely obliged, Petronella Ross

Auntie Lee and Grandma Almina as children, ca. 1914.

3

Reading Kierkegaard
Devotionally—A Memoir

One of the ways my mother weaned me from her immediate care when I was a child was by regularly securing for me a front seat on a Greyhound nearest to the bus driver for summertime trips. The destination was always the same: my mother's hometown of Story City, Iowa, 45 miles north of my own hometown. Story City also was where my only living brother and I buried our mother and father together in 2021. There, more than a half-century ago as I write this, I would play with cousins, sleep at the home of my then 60-plus-year-old grandmother Almina, and pay visits to my great-aunt Leora, whom I and other family members affectionately called Auntie Lee. Amid the many preadolescent bouts of boredom in their homes, I often thumbed through thin pages of small books with utter indifference. Daily devotionals all, they could be found on coffee tables, end tables, bedside stands, and kitchen tables.

During the first years of the COVID-19 pandemic that emerged at the end of 2019 and halted much of the world by mid-March of 2020, I found myself summoning up remembrances of those books. They were the size and age of books that sixteenth-century founding father of devotional literature Johann Arndt called "old, short little books that lead to a holy life." Palm-sized and psalm-centered, they kept quiet, steadfast company with Grandma Almina and Auntie Lee until the two died eleven-plus years after they each were widowed—all while sheltering in place much of their lives amid Iowa corn and soybean fields. It was at the advent of my own seventh decade, while the pandemic compelled my wife and me to stay close to home in our own little Midwestern village, that I began to understand why my Norwegian Lutheran matriarchs read those tiny tomes daily. Which brings me to three preliminary confessions:

• If church attendance across my adult years is any indicator of being a good Lutheran, I am a bad one.

• I had neither the slightest interest in nor curiosity about the essential nature or value of devotional literature until I began at the outset of the COVID-19 pandemic to reflect more deeply upon my great-aunt and grandmother's homes and lives.

25-year-old Auntie Lee with her groom,
Boyd Michaelson, and their six-year-old ringbearer,
niece Constance Egeland (my mother),
on their wedding day, July 1, 1933.

• Never before had I earnestly and deliberately thought to read the renowned nineteenth-century Danish Lutheran author devotionally in the strictest sense of that term—in other words, how I believe Kierkegaard wanted to be read.

I'll let my first confession be. Given that the second and third confessions bear directly upon the present discussion, the remainder of this section unpacks a few reasons for laying my heart thus bare, beginning with this question: Why would I ever feel a conscious want or need to read Kierkegaard devotionally?

More than 40 years of regularly reading, critiquing, admiring, and writing about Kierkegaard should speak for me as devotee. It is a designation about which I cannot think without also thinking of my dear wife, Jane, who has suffered my ever-competing devotion to Kierkegaard since before our marriage four decades ago. At that time, in 1984, I informed her that the only foreseeable financial liability I brought to our marriage was my personal vow to purchase the remaining books in Princeton University Press's pricey 25-volume *Kierkegaard's Writings* series (1978-98). Little did she and I know then that (and in addition to the cost of dozens of expensive one-volume monographs related to Kierkegaard studies) the even pricier 11-volume *Kierkegaard's Journals and Notebooks* series (2007-20) would eventually add to the debt. —This second series, incidentally, significantly altered the very way I read Kierkegaard, for to read its many pages through at least once, I began waking up an hour earlier every morning seven days a week to read a few pages—surely a devotional task.

Reading Kierkegaard regularly for more than 40 years did not mean, however, that I ever was reading Kierkegaard devotionally—which has something to do with reading him personally and privately…but also something more. Instead, I was reading his books mainly for external reasons that included a deep interest in Kierkegaard scholarship in order to prepare for essays, papers, lectures, and books on which I was working.

It was not until I began thinking of the nature of devotional literature amid that first year of the pandemic that I began to wonder if I nevertheless had been reading Kicrkegaard devotionally, yet only on some unconscious albeit minimal level, all along. Few have been the days in my adult life, in other words, when I did not find myself reading, thinking about, reflecting upon, and being instructed by something Kierkegaard wrote—something that, more often than not, directly related to how I was thinking about and living my life in the present moment. The more I awoke each day finding myself refracting the world and time's morning rays through Kierkegaard's prismatic writings, the more I began to detect value and meaning in even the least pale light or shade that came with each day's dawn. Was my reading fueled all along by something more than mere intellectual curiosity, personal literary enjoyment, and scholarship? Was my daily gift and task testimony to a more intimate, more private, more personal way of reading Kierkegaard? Reading devotionally is indeed a peculiar reading practice, for it is on the whole unsociable, obedient, and (worst of all to whatever scholarly or professional mask I still occasionally don) *uncritical.* Nonetheless, it also is one that I only recently have come to rank higher than reading Kierkegaard either personally or professionally.

There is also more to reading devotionally than just clocking regular time-on-task. Reading devotionally has, in addition, something to do with the speed by which the reader reads amid the task. Time, in this case, isn't meant to be an enemy that may trigger impatient anxiety wrought by worry over any given day's tasks; rather, time is reckoned as a friend that encourages patience for the sake of how best to reflect upon before ethically responding to what each day brings. Reading devotionally also has something to do with allowing time to render quiescent the reader's naturally divided attention (that sorry fundamental bane of being human that I, even now, transgress), so as to focus solely on receiving the message of the text…all in an effort to serve and attend to one "master" at a time instead of two. (In at least this context, reading, as a colleague of mine always reminded me, *is* rocket science.)

I am especially grateful to two people who exemplified this simple, difficult readerly tortoise-crawl. One of my two older brothers, John, read Kierkegaard in college at six pages per hour—not just out of an understandable undergraduate mystification over Kierkegaard's complicated syntax, but also for the author's clear and pure depth of thought of the world and time after the codes of syntax were cracked. There also was Kierkegaard translator Edna Hong's reading method: Just as Henry David Thoreau knew that books ought to be read as deliberately as they were written, Edna often said that the essential nature of truly good books was not that they were quick "page-turners" but that they *had* to be put down after turning one or two pages at a time to really read them. Only by putting them down could the reader move to reflect upon the pages turned and, in turn, be moved. Reading devotionally in this way has less to do with the number of pages consumed than with how a reader comes to appropriate ideas on each page slowly, quietly, and inwardly over time for one's own upbuilding.

After these technical practices having to do with regularity and speed and paying attention are considered, the reasons for reading devotional literature in general and reading Kierkegaard devotionally in particular begin to reveal themselves in contrast with reasons for reading Kierkegaard professionally and personally.

In his introduction to his 1941 book *Something About Kierkegaard*, pioneer Kierkegaard translator David Swenson offers a concise and compact personal sentiment that suggests a binary distinction between reading professionally and reading personally. He writes that, over years of reading Kierkegaard, he "found in his pages an increasing inspiration for the common tasks of life, as well as clearness and light upon a multitude of intellectual problems of the highest dignity, a matchless delineation of ideals in their ideality, as well as wonderful compass in the expression of humanly significant moods and feelings of every kind." Then he writes: "I should even like to say more than this," before concluding, "but I dare not…. Therefore I quit the dangerous ground of personal confession and pass over into the safer realm of objective narrative."

In the preface to her 1997 book entitled *Kierkegaard*, Julia Watkin speaks similarly, but weighs in more personally: "With Kierkegaard as a constant companion, I see ever more clearly his importance as one able to raise and address vital philosophical and ethical-religious questions about existence, raise them in such a way that his thought must be relevant to every generation. Surely few [authors] can be read so widely and avidly on both an interdisciplinary and an international basis. I am happy to count myself one of his readers and grateful for the opportunity to write about him."

In the preface to his 2019 book entitled *Kierkegaard and Spirituality*, C. Stephen Evans takes Watkin's personal affection a step further: "Although this may sound odd, I would also like to express my gratitude and my love for Kierkegaard. After fifty years of reading him and working on him, I find him as rich and profound as ever."

In the penultimate paragraph to her 2019 biography of *Kierkegaard, Philosopher of the Heart: The Restless Life of Søren Kierkegaard*, the tone of Clare Carlisle's personal testimony comes closer to Evans's testimony than to Watkin's or Swenson's:

> Kierkegaard remains endlessly interesting to me. This is because he spoke of, and to, a deep need for God within the human heart—a need for love, for wisdom, for peace—and he did so with a rare and passionate urgency. Though he relentlessly pursued "the task of becoming a Christian," he did not see this as a question of religious identity or affiliation. Perhaps he had too much disdain for institutional religion.... [or] more conventional Christianity. Through his authorship, which lasted barely more than ten years, he communicated infinite things from his own very human heart—in sparkling prose, with exceptional sensitivity and nuance, and with little trace of dogmatism or moralism.

31

Swenson, Watkin, Evans, and Carlisle reveal themselves not only as devoted readers professionally, but also personally—and not only personally, but perhaps devotionally in the strict sense of that term. These four scholars' testimonials further suggest that the borders between reading professionally, personally, and devotionally are not only distinct but permeable, and that a reader is capable of reading Kierkegaard, if not on multiple levels concurrently (an impossibility by some standards), then in rapid-fire succession contiguously.

All of which, curiously, reminds me of my Grandma Almina and Auntie Lee, not because either of them was a scholar (neither of them was, although Auntie Lee taught in a country school for a time) but because they were, in the words of Kierkegaard's pseudonym Johannes Climacus, "infinitely, personally, and impassionedly interested in their relation to this truth concerning their own eternal happiness." They also had witnessed and directly or indirectly suffered global catastrophes, including the 1918-20 flu pandemic (50 million dead), the Great Depression, and two world wars (73 million dead). I also suspect that they needed a way to attend to, reflect upon, and respond to the lives they found themselves living—lives of trials that were extraordinary in deeply personal ways amid their quiet, isolated rural farm community: domestic trials, the deaths of loved ones, the press of time, the unassuming and sometimes inscrutable pall that some silences bring to empty spaces in vulnerable hollows of the day. And so, by each of them simply making those books ever-present and accessible in an instant, in other words, by giving the devotional books they owned "a good home"—something Kierkegaard hoped would happen to his own books—my relatives sanctified those books, which meant giving the books special meaning by transforming them into something of great worth. In return for my relatives' quiet curatorships, the books themselves helped my relatives open up special meaning in their own lives by helping transform their lives into something of great worth. All Grandma Almina and Auntie Lee had to do was open up those books, read devotionally, then tend to very particular needs at any instant any time of any day.

For my grandmother and great-aunt, their number one need was a religious one, and it ranked above and before any personal needs they had. By Kierkegaard's way of thinking, such need is a person needing God, a need that he calls a human being's highest perfection.* It is a way of thinking about religious need with which, I suspect, my grandmother and great-aunt would have agreed. This need was

---

*Kierkegaard entitled one of his eighteen upbuilding discourses "To Need God is a Human Being's Highest Perfection," which Kierkegaard scholar Eduard Geismar calls "perhaps the most profound" of those discourses.

manifested in my relatives' homes as small, unobtrusive devotional books filled with words to which they became especially attentive, as Kierkegaard suggests, "every time human want and distress" made them "needful of comfort." It is a need, however, that may be unnerving—if not taboo—for many people living within a cultural milieu where religious belief and obedience to its precepts have long been waning "even in such a way," as Kierkegaard also suggests, "that basically it is shut out."

If, however, we are to begin to understand what Anti-Climacus meant when he spoke of "an anxiety about an unknown something or a something he does not even dare to try to know," it is difficult to ignore that (as he also writes) such a person "carries around a sickness of the spirit that signals its presence at rare intervals in and through an anxiety he cannot explain." And if we are to begin to understand what Johannes Climacus meant when he spoke of the happiness a person experiences when coming "upon one of the old devotional books and there quite rightly finding spiritual trial described," it is difficult to ignore the possibility of that person "having a deeply religious need."

Subsequently, the central religious aspect of Kierkegaard's authorship is to help make his reader aware of needing God, and that, according to Kierkegaard, "it is the saddest thing if a human being goes through life without discovering that he needs

God." For Kierkegaard, thinking about existing religiously is essential to what it means to be human. As difficult as it might be for any reader to comprehend what Kierkegaard means by existing religiously, primitive religious phrases such as *religious need* or *old devotional books* or *spiritual trial* that Johannes Climacus uses remain ubiquitous in and fundamental to Kierkegaard's religious lexicon. In one of Kierkegaard's indirect bids to make old religious things like devotional books new again, pseudonym Johannes de Silentio writes: "Should it be necessary for our age to have the ridiculous appearance of a [religious] enthusiast in order to find something to laugh at, or is it not rather more necessary that such an inspired character would remind it of what has been forgotten?"

Elsewhere, Kierkegaard's Johannes Climacus underscores how religious inwardness is an easily forgettable presupposition to what it means to become human when the practice of devotional inwardness is so easily hampered by ever-expanding caches of data and information that undergird but too often obfuscate knowledge. "My main thought," Climacus maintains, "was that, because of the copiousness of knowledge, people in our day have forgotten what it means *to exist*, and what *inwardness* is." He concludes with the sobering punchline: "If people had forgotten what it means to exist religiously, they had probably also forgotten what it means to exist humanly."

If devotional literature is intended to help readers exist religiously, then, readers become Kierkegaard's reader when they read with the kind of obedient wonder, generosity, and childlike openness of heart that Kierkegaard hoped readers would bring to his pages, what Kierkegaard scholar Frances Maughan-Brown calls "obedient reading, one that *believes* the text." Such trust and devotional receptivity by readers in turn allow readers to co-create with Kierkegaard the kind of existence in their own thoughts, words, and deeds that befit existing religiously and humanly.*

---

*The idea of co-creation here was inspired by the writings of and conversations with two Kierkegaard scholars, Frances Maughan-Brown and Sergia Hay. Co-creation is also what Kierkegaard himself arguably suggests in each of the six prefaces to the six volumes of upbuilding discourses that make up *Eighteen Upbuilding Discourses*. Each preface offers with minor variations his unchangeable desire to pass the baton of his creative thought over to the reader. The transfer prompts the reader to appropriate inwardly Kierkegaard's texts for the reader's own self in ways by which the reader may gain needed ethical inspiration to witness and participate in the world each day. Here are the six variations of Kierkegaard summoning up this co-creative spirit: "This little book [of upbuilding discourses].... finally [meets] that single individual whom I with joy and gratitude call *my* reader...who is favorably enough disposed to receive it.... [and who, like a bird] suddenly noticed it, flew down to it, picked it, and took it home, and when I had seen this, I saw no more" (*Eighteen Upbuilding Discourses*, 5); "...who by

In the end, reading Kierkegaard in the way he hoped to be read requires the reader's understanding of at least the possibility of a primitive religious need that abides quiescent within the reader, a need that may as of yet be unplumbed because the reader has yet to have honed the kind of receptive stillness and perceptive imagination needed to hear and see the need. Full access to Kierkegaard's wisdom also assumes that such a need, if unearthed or recalled, is subject to actual spiritual trial. As Kierkegaard's Johannes Climacus notes, "anyone who is not very religious will not be exposed to spiritual trials either,

---

making my thoughts his own does more for me than I do for him" (ibid., 53); "…who in receiving it…sanctifies [it], gives it meaning, and transforms it into much" (ibid., 107); "…who with the right hand accepts what is offered with the right hand…[and] who invests the humble gift to the benefit and joy of one who continually desires only to be as one absent on a journey" (ibid., 179); "…who takes an interest in the [discourse's author], gives an opportunity to what is said… [and] transforms the discourse into a conversation, the honest confidentiality of which is not disturbed by any recollection of the [discourse's author] who continually desires only to be forgotten…[and who] accomplishes the great work of letting the perishability of the discourse arise in imperishability" (ibid., 231); and that "this little book…. [which] seeks that single individual whom I with joy and gratitude call *my* reader…. is nothing for itself and by itself, but all that it is, is only for [the reader] and by [the reader]" (ibid., 295).

because spiritual trial is the response to the absolute expression of the absolute relation." Kierkegaard adopted Socratic methods of indirect communication to help readers become aware that the religious must at baseline be attended to in order to begin to imagine Kierkegaard's full concept of what it means to be a human being and, by extension, what it means to be *his* reader.

☙

I begin this section as I began the first, with a memory of a devotional text from childhood. This text is not one of the small devotional books discovered in my relatives' homes. It is instead a text from television, that default medium of so many kids like me growing up in the 1960s and beyond.

There is a moment in a beloved 1965 television cartoon Christmas special that is a fit analog to my experience of reading Kierkegaard devotionally. It occurs when, in *A Charlie Brown Christmas*, Charlie Brown learns the true meaning of Christmas through his friend Linus's measured, disarming, unsullied, quiet recitation of seven verses from the original Christmas story as reported in the Gospel of Luke. This *Peanuts* scene is rich with central Kierkegaardian motifs, including halting silence, the possibility of offense, a report of eternity crashing into time—all followed by characters' actions that intimate a humiliation, a presence of grace, and striving borne of gratitude, which is how Kierkegaard defines Christianity's essence.

If any fictitious character has been able to build a nest with confidence upon the sea like Kierkegaard's king-fisher, it is Linus. His calm and assured recitation of Christ's nativity, which silences and sobers and ultimately engages his audience to ethical response, carries a primitive, near-apostolic authority that confirms Johannes Climacus's words from *Philosophical Fragments*:

> Even if the contemporary generation has not left anything behind except these words, "We have believed that in such and such a year the god appeared in the humble form of a servant, lived and taught among us, and then died"— this is more than enough. The contemporary generation would have done what is needful, for this little announcement, this world-historical *nota bene*, is enough to become an occasion for someone who comes later, and the most prolix report can never in all eternity become more for the person who comes later.

In addition, Linus's devotional delivery mirrors Anti-Climacus's assertion that, despite or because of the possibility of offense, "all human understanding must come to a halt in one way or another, must take umbrage—in order then either to be offended or to believe." In the case of *A Charlie Brown Christmas*, the offense inspires the *Peanuts* gang one and all to, as George Pattison writes, "step out onto the public stage of active witness" by coming to Charlie Brown's aid in a time of acute despair and in the form of active and responsive neighbor love. Such responsive love, according to Kierkegaard, is how love builds up.

After reading Kierkegaard for more than forty years primarily as a Kierkegaardian—that is, academically, literarily, morally, theologically, esthetically, and in comparison with other writers and thinkers—reading Kierkegaard devotionally was and continues to be for me like how Charlie Brown in *A Charlie Brown Christmas* receives his friend Linus's words and deeds. It calms and centers; as Kierkegaard writes about youth's recollection of God's Word (which the *Peanuts* gang collectively experiences), it helps "where nothing else would help...: it breaks the spell of brooding seriousness [and]...disperses the fogs of busy care."

Reading Kierkegaard devotionally makes me feel like Charlie Brown in another way as well: Just as Charlie Brown was a skeptical but willing participant of commercialism's clamorous subversion of the original nativity story's silent night, I have long felt the compromising effects of being a skeptical but willing participant of academe's oftentimes objective, secular commentaries of that singular subjective religious thinker who is Søren Kierkegaard. Never having taught at the college level, I have never been a bona fide professor. Nevertheless, my decades-long book-writing endeavor as a Kierkegaard commentator does not exempt me from escaping the wrath that Kierkegaard (especially through his Johannes Climacus) directs at commentators and scholars whom he repeatedly identifies as *assistant professors*—a designation that, for Kierkegaard, equates with hypocrisy, double-mindednesses, and professional self-interest.

Even self-identifying as a "Kierkegaardian" holds little consolation. Kierkegaard would reject the designation out of hand as a sleight against his essential ethical message, which is to help readers become aware of their relationships not with him but with God, neighbors, and themselves ("Would that you in silence might forget yourself," Kierkegaard writes, "what you yourself are called, your own name, the famous name, the wretched name, the insignificant name..."). In addition, the assistant professor in me is an unabashed, sometimes-sick-unto-death paragraph writer of more objectively-driven writings that comment on Kierkegaard's more subjectively-inspired writings ("Would that in silence you might forget yourself, your plans, the great, all-encompassing plans, or the limited plans for your life and its future..."). On these counts alone, I am guilty of complicity in the vast publication apparatus of secondary literature on Kierkegaard that Kierkegaard scholar Howard Hong often worriedly dubbed the

"Kierkegaard industry."

Hong's worry is a paradox of sorts, for the "industry" of which he spoke always was and continues to be fostered by the very library that he and his wife, Edna, built up since the 1930s and gifted as a "Center for Research and Publication" at St. Olaf College in 1976. In that library, the Hongs conducted seminal research, oversight, and publication of English translations between 1967 and 1998 of the lion's share of Kierkegaard's journals and papers plus his published and unpublished works. Meanwhile, their exemplary personal industry went viral as the Hong Kierkegaard Library gained international traction as a scholarly destination. This expanded interested in Kierkegaard research and publication was in part due to the decades-long personal hospitality that the Hongs offered a long line of individual Kierkegaard students and scholars worldwide. In the end, their hospitality proved as formidable a legacy as the library they gifted to St. Olaf College, with that mantle of hospitality successfully passing to succeeding staff and curators to this day.

Howard Hong's worry, then, did not suggest any wish on his part to interfere with any scholar or general reader of Kierkegaard from researching and publishing on the Danish author's works, either out of a deep or impassioned understanding of his authorship, or out of a great gratitude for the author's achievements, or out of a desire to share critical understanding of Kierkegaard's wisdom to others. Rather, Hong worried about how a vast body of secondary literature might lure readers and scholars of Kierkegaard disproportionately away from Kierkegaard's primary texts—texts replete with deeply quiet, inward, and devotional messages having to do with understanding what it means to be a human being, what it means to need God and to love the neighbor as one loves oneself, and what it means to attend to one's own essential self that is located exclusively within one's own heart reckoned as ultimately broken and contrite. Even though, according to Kierkegaard scholar Kevin Hoffman, an occasional secondary Kierkegaard text may open up "whole new vistas," Hoffman prefaces this assertion by suggesting that reading swaths of secondary material on Kierkegaard can forestall a reader's professional, personal, or devotional engagement with Kierkegaard's primary text: "Readers regularly report what this is like, that point when secondary material, so initially illuminating, suddenly appears empty lying unfurled next to the original."

My position, then, either as Kierkegaardian or Kierkegaard commentator or unofficial assistant professor, is fraught. It perhaps becomes more fraught in my arguably hypocritical, double-minded, self-serving opinion that, either despite or because of Kierkegaard's blanket and relentless diatribes against my academic breed, most if not all of its more conscientious members survive on the hope that they help and not hinder a better understanding of Kierkegaard's thought and works in some modest way or another. It is with a sense of collegial commiseration, then, that I say I am not alone as I stew in this particular circle of scholarly hell that Kierkegaard, Dante-like, repeatedly stirred up for my ilk. Assistant professor Ryan Kemp's own confession is consoling, moving him as it does to a penitence in which he attempts to preserve his humanity by "becoming a better Assistant Professor" in a conscientiously ethical and ethical-religious context—or, if Kierkegaard's damning use of the professional designation cannot be shaken, by becoming "less of one."

Not officially being an assistant professor, my own confession on this score is still not unlike Kemp's: While not ignoring the possibility of and hope for repentance following remorse and confession, the inveterate backsliding commentator in me accepts Kierkegaard's judgment when he declaims, "Every commentator detracts.... *Pereat* the commentators! [Let them die!]" At least this assessment of my own paragraph- and footnote-writing career comports with the theme of the Jylland preacher's sermon at the end of *Either/Or* II in which there is something upbuilding in the thought that in relation to God, I—especially but not exclusively as a commentator—am always in the wrong (even now, especially now, as I write *about* reading Kierkegaard devotionally).

If any balm exists beyond my own guilt-con-
sciousness on this literary score, perhaps it is this: I
never feel greater joy than the occasional moment I
surprise myself by unwittingly reading Kierkegaard
in the way I can only describe as *devotionally*, that is,
in that wholly unacademic, obedient, silent, religiously oriented spirit that he wished to be received
by his readers. Under the spell of my objective, assis-
tant-professorial ways, his writings have been remarkable to me for many reasons, chief among them
his profound dialectics, his poignant lyricism, and
his ethical self-honesty. The inmost essence of why I
repeatedly have returned to him regularly over decades, however, is his unstinting communicative
power that stealthily breaks through the objective ar-
mor I subconsciously don every day to meet the
world and time—how, as he notes in one discourse,
I may come to sense a "resistance that does not follow the movements of the world's life," and that by
me letting that resistance "become more and more
pronounced" in me, my sense of being—call it my
soul—is thereby plumbed, touched, moved. Page after page, and even in his more patently esthetic
works, he quietly comes up from behind and am-
bushes my temporal being, always whispering not
only how I am not so temporal, worldly, and objective as I like to think I am most of the time, but instead how I am something more than temporal all of
the time. Herein lies my need to read Kierkegaard

45

not merely personally or professionally but devotionally, obediently, silently: he engages me in this communicative way especially but not exclusively in his religious discourses, wherein he seeks me out as (I paraphrase Kierkegaard here) *a single individual, to whom each book of his gives itself wholly, by whom it wishes to be received as if it had arisen in my own heart, that single individual whom he with joy and gratitude calls* his *reader, that single individual, who willingly reads slowly, reads repeatedly, and who reads aloud—for my own sake. If a book of his finds me, then in the remoteness of separation the understanding is complete when I keep the book and the understanding to myself in the inwardness of appropriation.*

Understanding only now in my early 60s that a relationship exists between reading Kierkegaard devotionally and unwittingly being surprised by reading Kierkegaard joyfully is not unlike how the elder Zosima in *The Brothers Karamazov* "marveled" when he himself discovered how "the simplest, most self-evident thoughts should come so late to our minds." I am further encouraged that St. Augustine did not take seriously the Psalms until his forties.[*] I am even further encouraged by Bob Dylan who, at age 79, penned in his Christianly evocative song "I've Made Up My Mind to Give Myself to You": "My heart's

---

[*] I thank Kevin Hoffman for reminding me of this fact in his lucid essay "A Reading Lesson" in *Taking Kierkegaard Personally.*

like a river, a river that sings/It just takes me a while to realize things."

In turn, this late-blooming revelation in me has compelled me to reflect upon less overt and more psychically subterranean origins of joy earlier in my life, and how such joy is linked to reading Kierkegaard devotionally later in life. I now finally understand what the Married Man of Kierkegaard's *Stages on Life's Way* understands when he maintains that "with respect to religion it is really true that one learns the best things as a child and acquires a presupposition that can never, never be replaced. A period comes later in his life when the impression of this piety almost overwhelms him. This is the crisis and is entirely in order."

઒

At the outset of the first section of this memoir, I invoked a childhood memory recalled at the beginning of the COVID-19 pandemic of my grandmother Almina and great-Auntie Lee's small editions of devotional literature that were available in most any room in their Story City, Iowa homes. At the outset of the second section, I invoked another childhood memory of a beloved Christmas story. These days, those memories support and inspire in a more concerted and concentrated fashion my own adult interest in reading Kierkegaard devotionally.

But there were other childhood events that contributed to my understanding of what it means to read Kierkegaard devotionally—events that have had no less an impact on me.

Far unlike the rigorous and deliberate religious orientation Kierkegaard received from his father, neither my mother nor my father engaged me directly or pedagogically about religion at home when I was a child. My mother was an old school mid-twentieth century conventional ELCA Lutheran. Whenever I heard Garrison Keillor's *News from Lake Wobegon* on the radio, I always imagined the main street and neighborhoods of my mother's hometown of Story City, that rural outpost and stronghold of Norwegian Lutheran pietism in Iowa, second only to Decorah.

As for my father, I still wonder if he ever earnestly believed in God—he told me as much during a conversation we once had about Freemasonry in Tolstoy's *War and Peace*, after he had spoken about how his father was a Freemason-turned-Unitarian. Nevertheless, my father always supported and participated in my mother's sense of churchgoing Lutheranism; during church services, he recited aloud and from memory the church liturgy, including the Lord's Prayer, the Nicene Creed, the Apostles' Creed, and the Brief Order of Confession of Sins and Forgiveness; he also sung all the hymns and always took Holy Communion. He also often enjoyed invoking the name of "George," which was his nod to the 1977 movie *Oh, God!* in which actor George Burns played the title role. In addition, and on the morning after my mother died, my then 90-year-old father came out of his bedroom singing an old Baptist hymn by heart (he later told me that he learned "Revive Us Again" during his boarding school days in Bell Buckle, Tennessee, so he had something to sing to his headmaster whenever he was in trouble).

Then there was the improbable story of my father's conversion to Lutheranism.

After the newlyweds settled in Des Moines and entered into the fold of St. John's Lutheran Church, my mother set up an appointment with the church's pastor, Rev. Louis Valbracht. According to my father, the appointment was made on an off-day, with absolutely no one in the sanctuary. When my mother brought my father into the sanctuary like she would later bring her three sons to Wednesday afternoon confirmation classes, Pastor Valbracht baptized my father on the spot, after which he gave my father a confirmation course in three minutes before pronouncing him confirmed into the Lutheran faith. Then, after pouring a full glass of communion wine and offering him bread and a sip of wine for his first communion, Pastor Valbracht let him polish off the glass, just like the pastors do.

I begin with this précis of my parents' religious orientations if only to underscore their minimalist approach to my initial religious orientation. It was an approach for which I was always grateful in that it allowed me to muster my own understanding of the religious more or less on my own.

I also am grateful that my parents never fostered enough religious hutzpah for the eye-rolling pre-adolescent in me to push against. Instead, they simply and matter-of-factly taught me and my two older brothers two prayers. The first was the seventeenth-century *New England Primer* bedtime prayer in which I, like so many millions of children, was unwittingly introduced to human finitude and the weirdly terrifying hope for God to take my soul if I died in my sleep on *that* particular night…and then the night after *that*…and the night after *that*! The second prayer was spoken each evening before supper. It was about God's greatness and goodness, that we thank him for the food, that by his hand we all are fed, then ending in a supplication for daily bread. In addition, they took me to church on Sunday mornings and, when I was a young teenager, Wednesday afternoon confirmation classes. Then, when I was confirmed, my parents gave me a copy of the Bible with my name engraved on its leather cover. —And that was just about all they wanted to say or do about me finding God or God finding me—except for one more thing, which had to with where I was to attend college.

Like a pre-arranged marriage, eventually the day came when my mother informed me that I would attend either St. Olaf College or Luther College. If I was not accepted into either of those two Midwestern bastions of Lutheran higher education, I was to attend Iowa State University, situated just south of my mother's hometown of Story City and to where I would have been grateful to have been accepted, for my high school academic records were lackluster. My applications to St. Olaf and Luther, however, were accompanied by recommendations from the senior pastor of my church (the very same who confirmed my father), which, I am all but certain, was why both colleges accepted my applications. I was too unformed and uninformed at that time to question the justice of the privileged status and lucky stars that a white, middle-class male such as myself had when it came to such matriculation. All I know is that it wasn't by the Grace of God that I was even offered the choice, nor was it by the Grace of God that I ended up at St. Olaf (*that* decision was made by Lady Luck late one Saturday night when I flipped a coin, which my two brothers witnessed: *heads* was the college that one of my two brothers attended, *tails* was the college attended by my other brother). —None of this would have happened, however, without my pastor's recommendations, and none of how my life unfolded after I arrived at St. Olaf College might have happened had it not been for my parents schlepping my brothers and me to church every Sunday.

∞

St. John's Lutheran Church is located in downtown Des Moines, Iowa. In its outdoor courtyard through which we always passed to gain entrance, a reflecting pool resides at the base of a larger-than-life replica of Bertel Thorvaldsen's statue of Jesus. Thorvaldsen's powerful, kindred *Christus* never ceased both to invite and halt me and so many other church-going children, just as I suspect that the original statue in Copenhagen behind the altar of the Church of Our Lady—along with the Matthew 11:28 fragment ascribed to it, *Come to me*—never ceased to invite and halt Kierkegaard. (The Church of Our Lady, incidentally, was the Kierkegaard family parish for Kierkegaard's whole life, this despite that the original church structure burned down amid a Napoleonic War bombardment by the British Navy in 1807, six years before Kierkegaard was born. The physical church was not fully rebuilt and open for worship again until 1829, which was when 16-year-old Kierkegaard entered it for the first time. As Kierkegaard biographer Clare Carlisle imagines the moment, the young man saw

> straight ahead of him, above and behind the altar, the [Bertel Thorvaldsen] figure of Christ himself.... [which] exuded gentleness and grace. His

head was bowed, his arms were outstretched and his hands open, and he stepped forward as if to meet his followers with his vast embrace. Somehow the gestures expressed a deep stillness. His quiet power was astonishing; he drew you in, but also brought you to a halt.

Carlisle's imagined depiction of the teenaged Kierkegaard is confirmed by the scores of times Kierkegaard refers to the Matthew 11:28 verse in his published work and journals, including a discourse in one book and a whole book section on the verse in another (with subsections entitled "The Invitation" and "The Halt"); he even alludes in another discourse to Thorvaldsen's statue itself: "At the altar the Savior opens his arms." The verse—"Come unto me, all ye that labour and are heavy laden, and I will give you rest"—may be the quintessential call to reading devotional literature devotionally.)

Aside from my parents teaching me two prayers and regularly dressing up my two brothers and me to go to Sunday church services, I am most thankful now for my parents' injunction back then that I regularly attend Wednesday after-school confirmation classes in my freshman year of high school.

The course was more than a supplement to my understanding of Sunday services and liturgical practices. It helped me understand a vocabulary that spoke not exclusively of this world and an ethical responsibility to it; it also spoke of a world beyond time and a deeper responsibility that includes an ethical-religious responsibility to existing in and mending the world while gaining an awareness that one is not essentially of this world. "Anyone who tells you that you can live only in time," poet Christian Wiman writes, "is not quite speaking the truth, since if we do not live out of time imaginatively, we cannot live in it actually. And if we can live out of time in our daily lives—indeed, if apprehending and inhabiting our daily lives *demands* that we in some imaginative sense live out of time— then is it a stretch to imagine the fruition of existence as being altogether outside of time?" Just as what Wiman calls *fruition of existence outside of time* may be a call to religious orientation, so, too, according to Wiman, "religion has always emerged at the edge of what humans know."

Kierkegaard speaks similarly of specifically Christian oriented vocabulary and upbringing when he speaks of the difference between ethical communication and religious communication: "the ethical, without further ado, is the universally human" whereas "there must first be communication of a little [religious] knowledge" for there to be religious communication, upbringing, and devotional "training" that commences "as in the ethical." Such knowledge need not be more than the brief précis of Christ's life as described in the Nicene Creed or the Apostles' Creed recited by so many churchgoers over the past two millennia (as Kierkegaard's Johannes

With my mother, Connie, at my confirmation reception in the courtyard of Des Moines' St. John's Lutheran Church. Behind us resides the church's replica of Bertel Thorvaldsen's statue of Jesus.

Climacus suggests) or as described in those verses from the Gospel of Luke as recited by Linus to so many church- and non-churchgoing television viewers over the past six decades.

The messenger of this religious communication and training was my confirmation teacher. He also was the senior pastor of the church I attended in my hometown (yep, the very pastor who confirmed my father more than two decades earlier and the one who wrote me college recommendations three years later).

Pastor Louis Valbracht was a larger-than-life, inviting-halting figure not unlike Thorvaldsen's *Christus* in the church's outdoor courtyard. To his young confirmands, this WWII Marine chaplain veteran who landed on Iwo Jima had a voice of New Testament compassion and Old Testament Abrahamic fear and trembling. He also had a stature and authority of the archangel Raphael or the prophet Jeremiah. If all that wasn't enough to get the attention of nascent adolescents, he fashioned—both in words and theatrical costume—Lenten sermons as first person accounts of contemporary witnesses of Christ, entitling them "I, Judas," "I, John," "I, Dismas" before performing as the biblical personages. On one Easter Sunday, he dressed as a Roman centurion and narrated his version of what may have gone through the soldier's mind as he ushered Christ to Calvary.*

In one of his more spirited sermons, Pastor Valbracht mounted the pulpit with a stack of *Penthouse* magazines, eager to defend conscientious printing press employees of the Des Moines-based Meredith Publishing Corporation, renowned for producing and publishing *Better Homes and Gardens*. The workers had recently objected to a new contract the corporation made with *Penthouse* to print the magazine for distribution in the upper Midwest, and Pastor Valbracht openly defended the workers on moral and ethical grounds. All I remember of the spectacle was that every member of the congregation sat bolt-upright in the pews and never once turned their heads to shelter their ears and eyes from witnessing firsthand the audacious sermon and pictorial spectacle. Years later, as a college sophomore, I read in Kierkegaard's *Either/Or* that Christianity brought sensuality into the world; then, reflecting back on that audio-visual exposé in which sin-consciousness met social injustice, I accounted Pastor Valbracht a genius for making sense of it all.

---

*For many years, Howard Hong had his ancient philosophy and Kierkegaard students develop similar first person presentations of great philosophers and Kierkegaard's pseudonyms, all to help students get the feel of the kind of passion that informed those philosophers and pseudonyms.

Pastor Louis Valbracht

It was, however, Pastor Valbracht as a confirmation teacher more than as a pastor for which I am most grateful. Like Kierkegaard, he respected his charges less as rote learners and more as fellow pilgrims. His pedagogical methods pointed to Christian and Lutheran dogmatics and creeds not by proselytizing but by philosophizing, and he was less preachy and more dialectical. He was also an avid reader of Kierkegaard himself, which I did not fully appreciate until after I had begun reading Kierkegaard in college and after my mother had reminded me of this; subsequently, Pastor Valbracht understood how Kierkegaard established dialectically distinct relationships between the eternal and time while simultaneously identifying the lynchpin that paradoxically connects the two *and* keeps the two separate: "It is of great importance for existence that in every generation there are existences each of which simply expresses the dialectical element," Kierkegaard writes. "Nowadays there are plenty of lives that express what is purely worldly—but we lack completely the one-sided and absolutely consistent expression of what is purely godly."

My two older brothers and parents revered Pastor Valbracht's reputation as an earnest and insightful instructor, so I wasted no time preparing myself. I purchased a brown, pocket-sized three-ringed binder in which I wrote notes that eventually included words and phrases like *the eternal, the absolute, ontology, teleology, ethics, and conscience; humans as* anthropos *(uplooker), as having a sense of responsibility and free will, and as having a sense of natural morality toward an understanding of the relationship between self, others, and God; humans as being able to question human purpose, origin, and destiny; arguments for the existence of God and the natural limits of those arguments; agnosticism, atheism, omnipotence, omniscience, holiness, justice, sin, sanctification; love as eros, philia, and agape; humans as a great contradiction to themselves; the creation story and other biblical stories as, above all, great parables by which to live; how parents can't give children godhood and how each human can have one of two gods, God or the human self; death and dying; guilt; Jesus Christ as both man and God; faith and grace borne of divine justice and love.*

When, in college, I compared notes that I took in my Kierkegaard course to notes I wrote in that tiny brown notebook (which had by that time become for me a sort of self-made devotional book in and of itself), connecting the dots between the religious, philosophical, and theological vocabulary that both Valbracht and Kierkegaard used was a cinch. I do not think that I would have come to remember and value my confirmation cache of religiously oriented vocabulary and ideas, however, had it not been for Kierkegaard helping me recollect and recall them in earnest. Similarly, I do not think that I would have much appropriated the message of the pledge I made after successfully completing my confirmation class—the one about believing in Jesus Christ as my divine Lord and personal Savior—without eventually recognizing how, as Kierkegaard scholar Habib Malik writes, Kierkegaard was always "busy tackling the question of how one becomes a Christian through a personal relationship with God, and [that] all his energies were devoted to that endeavor." — All of which confirms why Kierkegaard repeatedly wrote about how the great thought in Ecclesiastes (*Think about your Creator in the days of your youth*) "continually recurs, and sometimes later it will help you to think most naturally and best of the Creator," *and also* about how a person cannot simply "be content with thinking about your Creator," the latter of which points to a call or a summons to read and live devotionally, to regularly "exist in the truth one understands."

Incidentally, if my confirmation story is not unique, it also is still perhaps not entirely common. More common, I suspect, are readers of Kierkegaard who either have *not* been introduced to religious vocabulary and sentiment in their youth or who, having been introduced to religious vocabulary and sentiment, have lived lives that have neglected such vocabulary and sentiment. Kierkegaard, however, both acknowledges and anticipates this paucity throughout his authorship by presupposing that his readers either lack religious orientation or are to varying degrees secularly minded—otherwise, he would not have put such effort into his methods of indirect communication that place readers at least within earshot of the religious call to which he unendingly gives voice. His modest hope for readers who either lack religious orientation, are indifferent to such orientation, or are skeptical of the religious is that they at least may imagine the significance of his pseudonym Frater Taciturnus's admission. "I am not an offended person," Taciturnus asserts. "Far from it, but neither am I religious. The religious interests me as a phenomenon and as the phenomenon that interests me the most. Therefore, it is not for the sake of humanity but for my own sake that it distresses me to see religiousness vanish, because I wish material for observation." Kierkegaard's hope here is that the respect he regularly pays to a secular or non-religiously oriented readership (as evidenced by his Socratic commitment everywhere to try to meet the reader where the reader is) prompts each reader to give Kierkegaard's religious vocabulary at least a fair and honest dialectical look. For, if a reader is not willing to entertain the religious by orienting to the *communication of a little religious knowledge*, then that reader is not reading Kierkegaard the way Kierkegaard hoped his writings would be read.

Kierkegaard was a profound dialectician, moral philosopher, ethicist, esthetician, and prose lyricist;

he also was first-to-last a Christianly oriented religious writer, with his dialectics, moral philosophy, ethics, esthetics, and literary style all bearing the watermark of the religious. He wrote to help others arrive at the religious and then help each reader upbuild religiously. Readers or scholars who subsequently dismiss or ignore even the *observation* of the religious (in an effort, for instance, to make Kierkegaard more palatable to themselves personally or to their scholarly selves professionally or to their students in these secular times)—these readers or scholars fail to do justice to Kierkegaard's thought and writings, writings which presuppose a relationship between the eternal and the temporal that, for Kierkegaard, begins and ends with a human being needing God and the Absolute Paradox that is the God-man. "When the sphere of the paradoxical religious is now abolished or is explained back into the esthetic," Kierkegaard's pseudonym H. H. writes, "then good night to Christianity."

∝

Long after my thumbing through pieces of devotional literature as a child in the homes of my grandmother and great-aunt, and now equipped with some modicum of religious vocabulary supplied by my confirmation teacher, my second unwitting brush with devotional literature was the first unabridged Kierkegaard text I read. *An Occasional Discourse: On the Occasion of a Confession*—more popularly known as *Purity of Heart Is to Will One Thing*—was not unlike thoughts that Kierkegaard maintains a year later in his 1848 *Christian Discourses* as ethically and religiously wounding "from behind."

The edition I read then was the 1956 Harper Torchbooks paperback trade edition of Douglas Steere's 1948 revised English translation. I cite this bibliographical information because it was the trade edition that most of Kierkegaard's English-speaking readers would have known before the 1993 *Kierkegaard's Writings* edition was published. I also note this edition because the Gothic typography it employs in its section headings, not to mention the archaic pronouns—*thee, thine, thou*—in the text's opening prayer, all exemplify devotional textual intent of yore. The pronouns alone hint of what Steere writes in his translator's note to the volume's revised edition, namely, that the book is a "devotional classic" beyond compare in the nineteenth century. The typography, predating Luther by 300 years, also evokes pioneer Kierkegaard scholar Eduard Geismar's brow-raising 1927 opinion that nothing of what Kierkegaard has written "is to such a degree before the face of God. Anyone who really wants to understand Kierkegaard does well to begin with it."

I read Steere's translation of *Purity of Heart Is to Will One Thing* while sitting on a hard chair at a small table under a harsh study lamp just inside a big black door through which one gained entrance into the largely unlit Kierkegaard Library at St. Olaf College. (At the time, the Library resided on the sixth floor of Holland Hall, a campus building patterned after a segment of the darkly dramatic twelfth-century Romanesque fortress monastery of Mont St. Michel on the Normandy coast.) It was an utterly frigid Minnesota day in February 1979 near the outset of the second semester of my sophomore year, and I had formally begun the last Kierkegaard course Howard Hong taught before he retired from teaching and before he and his wife, Edna, committed the next 19 years of their lives to complete the 25-volume Princeton University Press *Kierkegaard's Writings* series. I had come to know that chair and table and lamp the month before, where I was invited by Hong to study during the January interim course that the then 66-year-old philosophy professor had taught for decades. The course was entitled Philosophical Ideas in Literature and included titles by T. S. Eliot, Albert Camus, Aldous Huxley, Arthur Miller, Henrik Ibsen, Arthur Koestler, Fyodor Dostoevsky, and Herman Melville. Along with my ninth grade confirmation course and three other philosophy courses in which I enrolled during my early college terms (Introduction to Ethics, Aesthetics,

Ancient Western Philosophy), the interim course was the perfect primer for reading Kierkegaard.

I began reading *Purity of Heart Is to Will One Thing*, then, as a devoted student and at approximately six pages per hour—as per the advice of my older brother, who took Hong's Kierkegaard course a few years before me. It was a reading speed that out of necessity I did not exceed; to this day, Kierkegaard's dialectically dense pages and complex syntax compel me to obey the speed limit. What I never will forget about this particular reading session, however, was the interminable length of time it took for me to read the opening two dozen pages. They were replete with lengthy articulations on sober themes of remorse, repentance, and confession—themes about which I knew little and cared less at the time. (My sophomoric ignorance left me clueless as to how careful Kierkegaard was foregrounding in those pages vocabulary and ideas that I would need later to meet the vicissitudes of my own heart.*) I also distinctly remember wrestling with my own impatience on every page to get to the central theme that the title implied—impatience that, as Kierkegaard suggests everywhere, does not mind being deceived (impatience that also, incidentally, forever looms, even

---

*In *Taking Kierkegaard Personally*, Kierkegaard scholar Peder Jothen aptly notes in a discussion of *Purity of Heart* that "the heart" of the discourse "really is about the importance of the doing the hard existential work prior to confession."

as I now write). Nor did I yet understand the tangled web of irony in which I was enmeshed: I was reading a book about the innumerable tactics that self-deception's avoidance employs to fuel the hypocrisy and self-serving nature of double-mindedness, the primary tactic being none other than...impatience. Yet another cruel irony also was lost on me when I finally, thankfully, gratefully beheld *twenty-seven pages into the book* the page in which the book's title was introduced, and where Kierkegaard almost glibly adds: "in a certain sense nothing can be spoken so briefly as the Good.... Oh, blessed brevity, oh, blessed simplicity, that seizes quickly what cleverness, tired out in the service of vanity, may grasp but slowly.... [and] at the cost of much time and much grief." I was, indeed, already too clever a student of impatience for my own good...and only getting better at it. Little did I know then that I was wrestling with a formidable devotional writer's discourse that would not be gainsaid. As Kierkegaard writes in another discourse: "If such a person does not want to understand himself, the discourse at any rate has understood him." Such is the power of patience undergirding all great devotional literature: it waits for the reader to understand it.

Subsequently, it was only much later that I more fully understood I was the kind of reader who was not yet the one Kierkegaard called *his* reader. Nevertheless, I was the kind of reader whom

Kierkegaard regularly enjoyed catching and releasing, the one stuck swimming in circles within swirling eddies of esthetic awareness, apparently unable to break through the liquid corridor into stronger and more meaningful currents of ethical and ethical-religious awareness. And so, there was never a text by Kierkegaard I remember reading more than *Purity of Heart Is to Will One Thing* in which I unwittingly suffered what the text was indicating I ought to and had to suffer, namely, an honest self-examination of the ways in which I had thus far in life tricked myself into ignoring or avoiding deeper and more fulfilling currents of self-awareness. (—Which leads me to yet another confessional aside: The word *ought* has often stuck in my throat, much like how the word *obedience* may stick in many people's throats, especially in my adolescent college years when I was less interested in obeying *oughts* and more interested in testing their limits. Only later did I come to understand that Kierkegaard's essential prescription for readers throughout his authorship is an ethical form of communication that he calls an "oughtness capability," one that in turn strives to obey the strictures of what he identifies elsewhere as "the boring categories of the good.")

When I eventually began to understand Kierkegaard's notable ethical springs and motives later in the semester course, the imprint of that first reading experience left me both terrified and exhilarated, of being "glad to the brink of fear," as Ralph Waldo Emerson would say. Howard Hong would later fittingly define the text as one that pounds "sand into every rat hole of self-deception." Page after page of my initial reading of that book, I examined my own artful rationalizations and false selves, my self-impressed witticisms laced with irony, not to mention other similarly constructed sophistries that had buttressed and reinforced the walls of my underground-undergraduate hole…even as I knew I was being cornered like a rat by the preeminent ratcatcher Kierkegaard. The entrapment, of course, is an ethical and ethical-religious one, deftly confirming what the young Kierkegaard suggests in his dissertation regarding how romantic irony is never the positive ethical or ethical-religious truth of acting and witnessing, but merely a negative way by which human intellect takes its first baby steps toward such ethical and ethical-religious revelation and truth. As Kierkegaard similarly suggests in a journal entry: "How true what Thomas à Kempis says…: 'do not become conceited about any art or knowledge, but rather fear for the knowledge that has been given you. For the more you know, the better you understand it, the more strictly you are to be judged if you have not lived all the holier.' Look, those were some words. One seeks knowledge, one strains all one's thoughts, one acquires it—and look, one has entrapped oneself."

After Kierkegaard pounded more sand down into my elaborate tunnel system with every turn of the page, I attended Hong's lecture on *Purity of Heart Is to Will One Thing*. With a raised eyebrow not unlike Mark Twain on the verge of a punchline, Hong (who looked like Mark Twain and had even performed as Mark Twain on occasion) noted that the book has *two* readers. Then came the punchline: the *solitary individual*. After a second too long, I got the joke: I am both indivisible and doubleminded, a coin with two sides, a head and a tail, a Jekyll and a Hyde, what Kierkegaard in one journal entry calls "a synthesis and thus naturally, if you will, a born hypocrite." I was indeed two readers: I was a conscientious individual existing anxiously alone with desperate thoughts while reading a book about the impossibility of serving two masters well; I also was an impatient 18-year-old punk distracted by a daily routine of unreflectively dissembling my humanity by fakery, by pretending to be something and someone I was not.

More terrified than exhilarated at the time, I began to feel like how a crime suspect might feel under the bald light hanging from the ceiling of a darkened interrogation room. I continued to sit long hours on that hard chair under that glaring study lamp while slowly coming to the frightful conclusion that I didn't want my life to continue to unfold as it was unfolding (not unlike existing one small level of consciousness above the frog that—unaware of its fate in a kettle of water that inconspicuously heats to a boil from room temperature—dies). I was terrified by the highly unlikely prospect of achieving anything close to what Kierkegaard dubs *purity of heart.* All of this fearful, yet also strangely exhilarating, remorse of conscience swirled about me…and I hadn't even finished my first reading of a complete Kierkegaard text! —Other Kierkegaardians, incidentally, have experienced similar fear and trembling over this text that Geismar figured was written "before the face of God." Peder Jothen writes of how he searched "for ways to stave off Kierkegaard's demand," while Amber Bowen recalls that, as a young scholar, "I did not want to hear what he had to say to me." Most "terrifying" for Bowen was Kierkegaard's particularly devotional idea of "surrendering to" and "resting transparently in" the power that, according to Anti-Climacus at the outset of *The Sickness unto Death*, created her—to float out "on the depths of 70,000 fathoms of water." Such encounters are Archimedean points whereby fearful existential levers help readers lift up their individual worlds into other spheres of existence, levers that Kierkegaard is always all too willing to invite his readers not simply to know, but to feel, experience, and suffer. "Your comfortableness, no, my dear reader, that I will not promote," Kierkegaard writes late in his authorship. "If you imagine that I am a [restaurant] waiter, then you have never been my reader; if you actually are my reader, then you will understand that I can even regard it as my duty to you that you be strained a little if you do not want the falsification and distortion, the lies and the slander, to wrest you the idea you have had about my serving something true."

By a simple twist of fate, I already was beginning to understand—if only as through a glass darkly—the essential importance of seeing myself more like how Kierkegaard and Socrates came to see themselves, as *suspicious characters*, or those who knew enough to know that they shouldn't so quickly believe everything they thought. Just as Dante, after having descended to the very depth of hell at the center of the earth, comes to find himself ascending again in a disorienting topsy-turvy moment, I experienced a fearful but still indistinct joy in the suffering that may visit a person amid such revelation preceding frank self-understanding and confession. It seemed to me, to quote Kierkegaard, "that there [was] something higher moving within me; I believe that I [could not] justify anything except continuing to serve it as long as possible." Continuing to read Kierkegaard to the point of reading him devotionally became for me "like that which happens when wing strokes of the wild bird, in being heard overhead by the tame birds of the same kind who live securely in the certainty of actuality, prompt these to beat their wings."

As much as I still all too often identify with the tame bird in me, it was in that very nick of time when things began to change; I came to understand, in other words, how an *actual, ethical* purity of heart necessitated not only fearfully suffering a broken and contrite heart, but suffering it repeatedly, even joyfully. Upon this first reading of mine of Kierkegaard, I read *Purity of Heart Is to Will One Thing* less how a budding student-scholar reads—that is, critically—and more how a human being with a budding sin-consciousness reads—that is, devotionally. To that end, *Purity of Heart Is to Will One Thing* compelled me to begin thinking earnestly about reading words and thoughts and ideas that Kierkegaard considers in another journal entry as reading and thinking *"for the sake of conscience"* wherein "a linguistic transformation... [or] the Archimedean point... moves heaven and earth"—which in and of itself is a pat definition of devotional reading. The very act of reading Søren Kierkegaard subsequently was akin to eight-year-old Helen Keller's famous first experience of suffering sorrow and repentance through the decoding of language and symbol. I slowly but eventually understood *Purity of Heart Is to Will One Thing* to be a piece of devotional literature whose goal and intent were to impact me less intellectually or academically and more devotionally and religiously. It was a book that Kierkegaard wrote to move a reader personally, inwardly, and daily. It was a text for personal upbuilding, self-examination, and awaken-ing—less for objective study and more to help the reader become human.

Although I now can say that I perhaps always have read Kierkegaard devotionally on some pre-cognizant level (I again attribute my brother John's simple six page-per-hour speed limit to slowing my reading down to a devotional crawl), the rising tides of academe and the workaday world already were advancing. "When one grows older," Kierkegaard writes, "the noise on earth makes it difficult to hear [God's] voice; and if one does not hear it, the noise on earth makes it easy not to miss it." Subsequently, such unconscious devotional reading of my first un-abridged text of Kierkegaard was quickly swamped by those tides, which compelled students like me to keep their heads above water for the sake of student scholarship, including criticism, essays, papers, lec-tures, and books. Any reader's first-time intellectual or devotional crisis is naturally unsustainable over time: "only momentarily can a particular individual, existing, be in a unity of the infinite and the finite that transcends existing," Johannes Climacus writes before concluding that "this instant is the moment of passion." Such singular moments exist as myster-ies briefly revealed, like when the tame birds are prompted to beat their wings when they detect the wing strokes of the wild bird overhead. Such revela-tions, according to Annie Dillard, are "less like seeing than like being for the first time seen…. when the mountains open and a new light roars in spate through the crack, and the mountains slam."

Ever since my first unwitting devotional reading of Kierkegaard, then, the unwitting or witting goal has been one of repetition—which, as anyone who has read Kierkegaard's pseudonymously penned *Repetition* knows, is not so easy to achieve. And although Bob Dylan sings that "you can always come back, but you can't come back all the way," a striving hope is part of the apparel that the devotional reader dons. "In a certain sense one devoutly comes backward to the beginning," Kierkegaard writes. "The beginning is not that with which one begins but that to which one comes, and one comes to it backward."

℞

It is, nevertheless, humbling to come backward to the beginning of things, to begin to read Kierkegaard devotionally after having trained my whole professional life to read him—as well as everything else in the world—with a geometer's critical eye intent on squaring as many circles as possible despite knowing the impossibility of achieving such results regarding at least the most important things in life. Just as the proverbial journey of a thousand miles begins with a single step, a slow half-hour devotional reading session repeated in regular and deliberate measure begins the backward movement to what Kierkegaard considers a more primary, primitive ethical and ethical-religious existence. It is a repeated movement that is meant to abjure whatever real or apparent authority that the assistant professor in me wielded for so long. Like Prospero at the end *The Tempest*, my job as a devotional reader is first to recognize whatever autonomy I have gained by harnessing "rough magic" from books (even devotional books), then to "drown" those books each day, to revoke my own bookish autonomy I gain by those books each day—all in an effort to maintain a fundamental humanity and personhood, to step out (as Pattison writes) *onto the public stage of active witness*. There are, in other words, more things in heaven and earth than are dreamt of when one's nose is in a book. Closing books to *go and do likewise* is as essential to a devotional life as opening them in the first place.

What Johannes Climacus writes in his *Postscript* about revoking books and immersing oneself in existing applies here. His critique of book learning is not so much about wholly excluding books from one's life but rather about subordinating them in the individual's life—especially so that the individual can in fact exist, which means not simply to live biologically but *to stand out*, to take a stand *ethically* (from Latin *existere* 'come into being', from *ex-* 'out' + *sistere* 'take a stand'). "Scholarship is wholly legitimate," Climacus writes—

> On the other hand, one gets no unalloyed impression of critical… scholarship. Its entire effort suffers from a certain conscious or unconscious duplexity. It always looks as if something for faith, something pertaining to faith, should suddenly result from this criticism. Therein lies the dubiousness…. But it in no way follows that I am now supposed to build my eternal happiness on this book, which concludes…. ergo, now you can build your eternal happiness on these writings…. What is needed…is merely a dietetic precaution, a renunciation of every learned intermediate clause.

My confession here is also humbling because it is hard to confess that my wayward ventures into scholarly academic criticism—well-intentioned and for the good, as I always have hoped these ventures have been and continue to be—nevertheless are forever doomed to smack more of refutation or negation than confirmation. Why attempt to square circles in the first place? Why not yield to Robert Frost's words when he writes that "we dance round a circle and suppose,/But the Secret sits in the middle and knows"? Is the professional critic's will and imagination doomed to duplexity, as Johannes Climacus suggests?

It is humbling, then, to come backward to the beginning of things. It is humbling because it is difficult to unlearn the scholarly, to walk it back, as it were; to retract the very professional path that has sustained me and my ego for so long while nonetheless asking again the age-old ego-stripping questions of place (*Where am I?*), origin (*Where did I come from?*), destiny (*Where am I going?*), identity (*Who am I?*), and purpose (*Why am I?*), not as a scholar or critic or commentator this time, but as a penitent and a pilgrim; to decrease what I have for so long increased; to become like a child again; to say things that perhaps one only says in church on Sundays amid exchanges with peers and pastors; to obey. In this sense, the walk-back is simply a movement toward the religious and, as such, a devotional movement of humility amid spiritual trial or, in the old religious sense of the term, a movement of humiliation and thus one that is not merely difficult but...terrifying. Kierkegaard notes:

> An old, time-honored, and trustworthy devotional book[*] declares that God deals with a human being as the hunter deals with game: he chases it weary, then he gives it a little time to catch its breath and gather new strength, and then the chase begins again. Is it not acting like a hunter for a devotional book to shock in this way: by its name to invite people to the composure of the upbuilding and then to startle them? And yet this is quite in order, and we

---

[*] The Hongs note that this book is Johann Arndt's *True Christianity.*

shall receive the upbuilding. Woe to the person who wants to build up without knowing the terror; indeed, he does not know what he himself wants!

Perhaps, then, in my initial reading of *Purity of Heart Is to Will One Thing*, I merely received a foretaste of suffering this kind of terror that Geismar suggested when he wrote that nothing of what Kierkegaard has written *is to such a degree before the face of God*. Such terror is not entirely incommensurate with Johannes de Silentio's terrifying, repeated thought in *Fear and Trembling* wherein the knight of faith is the person capable of establishing an absolute relationship with the absolute. I know myself to be, however, still a million miles away from such *truly* terrifying moments in a life. Instead, what I find myself speaking of even now is the idea of facing the local and admittedly pedestrian terror of reading Kierkegaard devotionally as a merely quiet and solitary practice before attempting day-in and day-out to live on the basis of that devotional truth as best as I can, to *go and do likewise*—a task and a gift that, especially for readers like me who double as assistant professors, is terrifying enough. Writes Kierkegaard:

> We have invented learned scholarship in order to avoid doing God's will. For this much we surely understand: that face to face with God and with respect to his clearly understood will, no one dares to say "I won't do it." We don't

dare do it that way. So we protect ourselves by making it appear that it is difficult to understand, that we therefore…study and research, etc.: that is, we protect ourselves by hiding behind big books.

ભ

When Blaise Pascal maintains that "the sole cause of man's unhappiness is that he does not know how to stay quietly in his room," I suspect that he wasn't advising that everyone live out the happy fantasy of the introvert-scholar by quietly holing up alone in a room to conduct scholarly work. Rather, I suspect he was talking about the need humans have, whether they know it or not, to forswear so many diversionary tactics that they naturally perform during most of the minutes of their days so as to avoid coming face to face with the absolute. Such diversionary tactics compel satirist Kierkegaard to aver how "there are millions who perhaps have scarcely an extra half-hour a year in which to think about their inner lives."

Describing in a nutshell the near-infinite damage that continuous diversion can create, Kierkegaard transcribes words in a brief journal entry from the twelfth-century French theologian, mystic, and devotional writer Bernard of Clairvaux: "'That soul which is occupied with other things cannot replenish itself by God's visit.'" Bernard of Clairvaux's words stand alone in that journal entry without any commentary by Kierkegaard. It is as if Kierkegaard wanted to attend devotionally to Bernard's words alone—without, that is, even the distraction of constructing his own objective thought on the sentiment. Perhaps Kierkegaard stopped writing to direct his full devotional attention to God's visit at that very moment, that passionate purity-of-heart finite/eternal instant to which Clairvaux's words speak and that manifestly wills only one thing. Perhaps Kierkegaard knew that Bernard's words could stand as epigraph to what Kierkegaard spent much of his life writing about, namely, how the rapidly modernizing, highly inventive and bustlingly entrepreneurial nineteenth century world and beyond demands so much of our attention, all to the exclusion of so many other things that otherwise demand hard-won devotional time and interest in daily life—things like reflection, understanding, inwardness, imagination, will, passionate engagement, personal encounters with others, silence, humility, contrition, earnestness, to say nothing of needing God. The very practical activities of reading and thinking devotionally before living a devotional life, then, are terrifying enough for anyone who attempts to forswear such diversions. As much as Kierkegaard himself read and wrote devotional literature regularly amid his own attempts to live in the truth that he understood, even he confesses: "I wish to God that my own life were as pure as my authorship is profound and unselfish." This 1848 entry presages a concluding note in "The Accounting" of *On My Work as an Author* (1851), which asserts that "this is how I *now* understand the whole [of my authorship]. From the beginning I could not quite see what has indeed also been my own development…. I [now] regard myself as a reader of the books, not as the author." (It is also no wonder why Kierkegaard would read aloud his drafts when revising them and why he repeatedly asked his readers to do the same with the published versions. He did not simply aim to assure proper rhythm, flow, and cadence to the texts by reading them aloud. He also knew that declaiming is how a reader lays claim to and assumes the role of the first person narrator—by giving, like a good actor, actual and compelling voice and utterance to each persona, by "taking on another's role" so as "to acquire a sort of surrogate" for the reader's own life.)

෧

In his religious discourse *Purity of Heart Is to Will One Thing*, Kierkegaard writes that the discourse

> is asking you, then, or you are asking yourself through the discourse: *What kind of life is yours; do you will one thing and what is this one thing?…* Do you will one thing in truth?… Before being able to answer this earnest question earnestly, a person must already have

chosen in life, chosen the invisible, the internal; he must live in such a way that he has hours and periods in which he collects his mind so that his life can attain the transparency that is a condition for being able to submit the question to himself and answer it—if what I suppose is correct, that for this it is required that one must know whereof one speaks.

Author Robertson Davies speaks similarly in a 1973 speech to students attending Canada's oldest day and boarding school for girls. He advises his young charges to forget the ephemeral happiness found in diversion and instead pin their hopes on understanding that "the good life is not lived widely, but deeply" and that not just doing things but understanding what they do is what matters. In effect, Davies calls for devotional practice, especially if reading and thinking and acting devotionally means to attempt to begin to live in the truth one understands. "What you must do is to spend 23 hours of every day of your life doing whatever falls in your way, whether it be duty or pleasure or necessary for your health and physical well-being," Davies says. "But—and this is the difficult thing—you must set aside one hour of your life every day for yourself, in which you attempt to understand what you are doing." Then comes the terrifying:

Do you think it sounds easy? Try it, and find out. All kinds of things will interfere. People—husbands, lovers, friends, children, employers, teachers, enemies, and all the multifarious army of mankind will want that hour, and they will have all sorts of blandishments to persuade you to yield it to them. And the worst enemy of all—yourself—will find so many things that seem attractive upon which the hour can be spent. It is extremely difficult to claim that hour solely for the task of understanding, questioning, and deciding.... [but] the remedy usually lies in your own hands.

The kind of quotidian remedy to which Davies refers is arguably found only in devotional solitude, in shutting oneself up in one's room, in entertaining the monastic category of eternity instead of merely the social categories of the world and time. It is a prescription that is something by which the diversionary mind is terrified most of all. It is, according to Pascal, "why prison is such a fearful punishment," and something upon which Kierkegaard also comments:

It is a frightful satire and an epigram on the temporality of modern times that nowadays the only way people can think of using solitude is as a punishment, as prison. What a difference from the times when—regardless of how worldly temporality has always been—people nonetheless believed in the solitude of the monastery, when people thus revered solitude as the highest thing, as the category of eternity—and now people avoid it like a curse, so that it is only employed as a punishment for criminals. Alas, what a change.

For, what are acts of such monastic-like devotion to solitude, especially acts committed to reading and thinking devotionally, if not terrifyingly silent, unsociable acts of trying to step back from a busy world if only to attempt to understand oneself and what one is doing day-in and day-out? (Mark Twain was right: *Be good and you will be lonesome.*) For any striving devotional reader with whom, according to Kierkegaard, "one associates sociably-diffusely without essential inwardness and with more or less indifference," Kierkegaard knows precisely what is at stake: "the smaller the number becomes, the less social…the association becomes, that is, the more inward it becomes, the more an either/or begins to become the law for the relationship; and in the deepest sense the association with God is unconditionally unsociable." (The more sociable Judge William in *Either/Or*, incidentally, considers how the unsociability of an individual's God-relationship plays out amid a congregation in church, even as he rightly suggests that such a relationship may deepen one's relationship with others:

> The religious has a tendency to isolate the individual…. [and] that even though in a certain

sense one receives the impression of a congregation, yet the individual feels isolated; people
become strangers to one another, and they are
united again only by way of a long detour, as
it were. And what is the reason for this except
that the individual feels his God-relationship
so powerfully in all its inwardness that beside
it his earthly relationships lose their significance? For a sound person this moment does
not last long and a momentary distancing like
this is so far from being a deception that instead it augments the inwardness of the earthly
relationships. But that which as an element can
be sound and healthy becomes a very grave
sickness if it is developed one-sidedly.

For Judge William, then, the real terror of experi-
encing a God-relationship occurs if it becomes so
protracted that the individual eschews Christ's call
for neighbor love.)

As much as Kierkegaard knew that diversionary
activities such as "vacation trips to a spa" offer socia-
bly accommodating methods when "treating man as
spirit," he still believed that it was "fortunate, after
all, that we have the old devotional books to hold
to," for, "how in the world would we acquire these
mental states in our age." Unpopular and unfashion-
able as the thought of reading such devotional books
quietly in one's own room is—especially amid these
hyper-digital, hyper-diversionary, hyper-self-focused
times—Kierkegaard envisions the very heart of the

problem while offering a way to think about reading such literature by thinking about what, at its very heart, religiousness is:

> The result of busyness is that an individual is very seldom permitted to form a heart. And on the other hand, the thinker, the poet, the religious person who has actually formed a heart never becomes popular, not because he is difficult but because it requires quiet and protracted work and a confidential relation to oneself as well as seclusion…. Religiousness… is in fact about talking softly with oneself.

◌

I end this chapter with a note of thanks as well as with some of my own concluding remarks regarding reading Kierkegaard devotionally—all before giving Edna Hong, in a discussion of her devotional reading practices, the last word.

In my efforts to read Kierkegaard devotionally and to write about reading Kierkegaard devotionally, I am nothing but grateful to many Kierkegaardians of different orientations—secular, political, cultural, and religious—who (to quote Kevin Hoffman again on the advantage of reading secondary literature) have helped open up "whole new vistas" for me to consider through their own secondary literature. In particular, one scholar's book helped inspire the composition of the present text while another scholar's book helped me continue to work on the text.

Just before the pandemic made itself known globally in March 2020, I had finished reading Frances Maughan-Brown's 2019 *The Lily's Tongue: Figure and Authority in Kierkegaard's Lily Discourses*. Maughan-Brown offers a close reading of 14 religious discourses by Kierkegaard that were all inspired by the same 10-verse passage from the Gospel of Matthew (6:24-34), wherein Christ's Sermon on the Mount invokes lilies and birds.* One of the many things that her book offered me was the invitation to reread these 14 devotional pieces not as a scholar would read them professionally and objectively but as a devotional reader would read them at a time of great worry, suffering, and trial in our world and thus more in the spirit in which Kierkegaard would

---

*These discourses were published between 1847 and 1851 by Kierkegaard in four different publications, and may be located in the following volumes in the *Kierkegaard's Writings* series: *Upbuilding Discourses in Various Spirits*, 155-212 (three discourses under the title "What We Learn from the Lilies in the Field and from the Birds of the Air"); *Without Authority*, 1-45 (three 1849 discourses under the general title "The Lily in the Field and the Bird of the Air: Three Devotional Discourses"); *Christian Discourses*, 3-91 (seven discourses under the general title "The Cares of the Pagans"); and *Judge for Yourself!*, 145-213 (one discourse under the title "Christ as the Prototype, or No One Can Serve Two Masters").

hope his reader to read those discourses. Then, well into the composition of this book, Sergia Hay's 2020 *Ethical Silence: Kierkegaard on Communication, Education, and Humility* helped me realize all the more deeply how silence—both ethical and aural—is central to the very nature of devotional reading and to ethical responses toward the neighbor to which reading devotionally ultimately points.

In addition, each author indicated to me in her own way an abiding respect for the kind of supra-personal, religiously oriented, subjectively focused, obedience-based approach that Kierkegaard invites his readers to practice amid slow, sustained silent reading sessions. Then, in close re-readings of Maughan-Brown's and Hay's texts, their books came to look less like secondary literature to Kierkegaard's writings and more like primary texts in and of themselves, akin to how Kierkegaard's books are primary texts even as they are devotionally oriented secondary texts responding to primary sacred text.

In the end, the present book was initially prompted by how so many people began to shut themselves behind doors at the outset of a pandemic, the likes of which the world hadn't seen since the 1918-1920 influenza pandemic. I was also inspired by the isolation that my grandmother, Almina (b. 1905), and my great-aunt, Auntie Lee (b. 1908), must have felt not only in their childhood years during that infamous pandemic but also well into their later years.

Visiting with Auntie Lee in 1992,
three years before she died.

I was further inspired by the memory of devotional books owned by my grandmother and great-aunt, which were placed on end tables, kitchen tables, coffee tables, and bedside tables of their rural Iowa homes, thereby remembering again my creator in the days of my youth. I was, in addition, inspired by reading the devotional works of Kierkegaard translator Edna Hong (b. 1913), yet another matriarch with whom I came to appreciate deeply and to whom this book is dedicated and on whom this book's final chapter focuses. —As much as all of these people and places and events have moved me to read Kierkegaard devotionally, Maughan-Brown and Hay's books in turn confirm for me the hopeful, obedient, slow, silent, unsociable, narrow path upon which devotional reading requires of the lay reader and scholar alike if that person aspires to walk in ways that reopen doors of being, especially doors in which one may ethically and religiously respond to the summons to which devotional reading calls the reader to attempt each day. Reading devotionally is ultimately a way of reading in which acceptance of (to the point of, as Maughan-Brown maintains, *belief in*) the message of the text informs an active response of obedience and imitation, a movement from reflective will to an active faith played out daily in words and deeds ethically communicated to oneself and to others. If Kierkegaard's famous sentiment about *understanding life backward* involves a certain third person objectivity to accommodate human understanding, then his equally famous sentiment about *living life forward* requires shedding the skin of the objective third person to reveal religiously the subjective first person and in the direction of the devotional, the faithful, the simple—all pointing to the very essence of why Kierkegaard wrote devotional literature for people to read in the first place.

Reading devotionally means practicing obedience, which requires, as Hay suggests, not only the necessary silence of religious faith, but also the ethical silence that "prioritizes actions over words" that, with Christ as an exemplar, one comes to love the neighbor as one loves oneself. —All of which is something that Edna Hong, echoing Søren Kierkegaard, suggests everywhere in the next chapter when she speaks of existing in the truth that she came to understand, an existence shaped in great part by her reading Kierkegaard devotionally.

4

Edna Hong Reading Kierkegaard Devotionally

Only a few times in Edna Hatlestad Hong's published writings does she directly name the person to whom she was married for two months shy of 70 years. Instead, she identifies him simply as *my partner* or *my companion*. Subsequently, anyone unacquainted with the couple's shared life could conclude that they may have lived more apart than together. That conclusion, however, would only tell a half-truth. A more just conclusion would suggest that Edna and her companion both had long appreciated Rainer Maria Rilke's suggestion that an enduring and interdependent trust between marriage partners presupposes an endearing protection of the solitude and independence of the other. "Once the realization is accepted that even between the *closest* human beings infinite distances continue to exist," Rilke writes, "a wonderful living side by side can grow up, if they succeed in loving the distance between them which makes it possible for each to see the other whole and against a wide sky!"

At the beginning of many of Edna's lectures and interviews, one such extraordinary feature is salient, redefining as it does with levity the very constitution of their initial marriage contract. The same joke always seemed new when Edna spoke of unwittingly turning bigamist by tying the knot with her partner. In one interview, she remarked: "When I married Howard Hong in June of 1938, I had no idea I was marrying *two* men."

Later in the interview, Edna noted that Søren Kierkegaard (the other man) "was a genius. And he had so much to write that he *had* to, he simply *had* to have time and solitude and privacy."

Interviewer Bo Elbrønd-Bek then asked: "But you raised *eight* children! And...."

Edna: "Yes, well, we're not geniuses, though, and..."

Bo: "And sitting at your kitchen table, translating, and also writing your own books."

To this, Edna offers an intriguing qualification: "Yes, but that's not number one, you see. That's not the passion, the number one passion, in our lives—at least not in *mine* anyway. But seriously, and I have said this before, I would go *mad* if I did Kierkegaard all day. I would go *mad* if I did housework all day."

In Edna's vernacular, *passion* was the old religious kind, the one that denoted a psychical suffering, a painful longing *for* in conjunction with an earnest devotion *to* something immediately perceived as absent from one's life. When she designated a particular passion as *number one*—one under which all other passions were subordinated—she quickly realized that she waded into a topic that may be too personal or subjective a tale to tell amid an interview that focused more outwardly on the topic of "Kierkegaard in America" and, specifically, the Hongs' translations of the Danish author. So, she redirected the focus (again with levity) onto the prospect of *going mad* translating Kierkegaard all day every day or *going mad* carrying out her post-WWII wifely duties as head housekeeper all day every day. Her number one passion disappeared and was not further elucidated in the interview. Despite Edna marrying in an era when, according to another Hong interviewer, "married ladies were expected to devote themselves to their husbands' careers," and despite so many other ongoing secondary passions of hers (composing first-draft English translations of thousands of pages of the writings of her *other* husband; writing and publishing more than a dozen of her own books that arguably are all devotional in nature even as they are clothed in different genres ranging from the short story, the novel, memoir, and historical fiction; raising eight children plus conducting the housework required to help sustain and manage her children and her husband's domestic worlds)— despite all these passions, Edna's number one passion was nevertheless revealed indirectly in that interview as a sacred, silent absence akin to what George Steiner calls *real presence.*

In her books, Edna's number one passion also surfaces and disappears, albeit in more crafted and deliberate ways, thanks in great part to her literary acumen that regularly attempted to express the nature of ineffable longing. In narrative genres other than the interview, Edna more confidently unspooled her number one passion in ways a reader might more openly receive and understand the object of her passion. In her memoir of her rural Wisconsin childhood, for instance, she speaks of how "something was communicated to me by the church in my home and the church in my community…. [wherein] my life was set in perspective to time and eternity, to the temporal and the eternal. Before longing, man's umbilical cord to the eternal, could dry up and dissolve from disuse (although I do really believe this is totally impossible), the numinous-arousable me was set in relationship to him who planted the numinous-arousable in me." Then she directly names the object of this passion of hers before it recedes into the narrative's background (not unlike the very nature of the object of passion itself):

> Oh, God did not shout his presence to me. Instead of experiencing him as the Hound of Heaven, as did Francis Thompson, I experienced him more as Philip Toynbee does, more

in the "guise of a very shy rabbit, constantly disappearing down his hole." What the church in my home and the church in my community did was to develop a potential planted in me into a condition of mind and spirit that acknowledged the presence of God.... So I thank my parents for not placing me painfully outside the church but inside, where the Word could get at me.

Edna's primary passion also surfaces in formative moments of the lives of historical and fictional characters that people her books. The narrator of her historical novel *Bright Valley of Love* speaks of fledgling intimations of spiritual awakening that visited the young and severely disabled Gunther, the book's protagonist:

It was as if [Gunther had] received a telegram from another world. It was quite another message than the ones he got through the window from the ringing of the church bells and the clatter of horses' hoofs and cart wheels on rough cobblestones.... It was as if someone or something was trying to inform him of something he ought to know. As if a presence was trying to push into a great absence. Something secret, wonderful, too big to grasp.... It was a telegram from another world of something unknown. Yet it was not a banner of pure joy, for it seemed to be telling him also of something missing. Not something lost, but of something he had never had.

In her last book, *Box 66, Sumac Lane: A Lively Correspondence on Sin and Sanctity* (1989), Edna's passion is revealed through the life of Molly Mortenson, the protagonist that Edna makes clear is not unlike its creator in two intimate ways: Molly is a devotee to and also a translator of Kierkegaard. Below, Edna has Molly's editor Tate Kuhlman help Molly to see how all her work on the concept of sanctification—the call to be holy—has led her to become who she is: "Do you realize, Molly, that you have consciously or unconsciously made a shift in your concerns about the subject of sanctification?" Kuhlman asks. "One could whimsically call it an about-face. Before your disappearing act you wrote *about* sanctification, *about* the call to be holy, *about* becoming what we already are. Now you express a longing to see the fruits of holiness hanging from the branches of the tree that is your own Molly-self."*

Here, Tate acts as Socratic midwife, helping Molly give birth to something that she already knows and understands. It is something that she already recognizes as Kierkegaard's concept of a

---

The longing to see the fruits of holiness hanging from the branches of the tree echoes a sentiment from Kierkegaard's *Works of Love* that Edna and Howard long held dear regarding what it means to be human—how, that is, "the tree is to be known by its fruits."

genuine human existence, namely, to begin "to exist in the truth one understands" (a concept to which Molly herself referred some 65 pages earlier); it is also something that, elsewhere, Edna calls existing "in the truth of the day, and [that] even if you know only a smidge of that truth, you exist in that smidge."

What the remainder of this chapter suggests is that Edna Hong reading Kierkegaard less professionally and more devotionally—as exemplified in her words and deeds above and below—serves as hints of her number one passion: a passion that regularly surfaces as much in her personal life as her literary life. It is a passion that finds meaning not only in her own deepest silences and moments of emptiness but also in her daily attempts to make manifest her most *secret, wonderful, too big to grasp* unknowns in ways that regularly revealed her as existing in the truth that she came to understand. It is ultimately a passion to reconnect with a holiness with which she believes she was originally endowed, a longing to see the fruits of holiness hanging from the branches of the tree that she believes was her own Edna-self. It is also the number one passion that Kierkegaard hoped his authorship would awaken in individual readers like Edna, that is, the longing and ability "once again to read through solo, if possible in a more inward way, the original text of individual human existence-relationships, the old familiar text handed down

from the fathers." Edna once noted how her authorship had been influenced by Kierkegaard: "Kierkegaard comes out in almost everything."

∞

Edna Hong reading Kierkegaard devotionally, however, did not occur without her suffering obstacles
that conspired against the very act of reading devotionally, obstacles that were created as much by
scholarly predilections of her lawfully wedded husband as by personal prejudices of her other husband.

She must have pitied her companion, for instance, when she witnessed him writing footnote after footnote for the scholarly apparatus of their co-
translations, which included the seven-volume Indiana University Press *Søren Kierkegaard's Journals and
Papers* series and 21 volumes of the 25-volume
Princeton University Press *Kierkegaard's Writings* series. Edna's pity for Howard in this respect also must
have occurred often, for he wrote more than 23,000
footnotes ranging from one-line to multi-page cita-
tions. Surely she chuckled when translating the following quip from Kierkegaard's journals—"the
learned people are forever producing learned works
and losing themselves in footnotes"—before passing
it on to Howard to proofread and to write its cita-
tion. (As for Howard, he seldom complained of this
immensely valuable scholarly work about which he

was fiercely passionate and around which he created a formidable working library, one that then housed some 20,000 print volumes, 6,000 journal and newspaper articles, 570 print-volume dissertations, plus online sources, films, and videos. One day, however, while trudging up the six floors of stairs to St. Olaf College's Holland Hall attic where the Hong Kierkegaard Library originally was perched, I heard him bemoan that he had become nothing more than a writer of footnotes. It was a fate with which he presumably had not fully reckoned at the start of it all, this seemingly unending attention to scholarly detail after scholarly detail, this miniscule writing event repeated over and over again and again, this 60-plus-year meander on some Dantean hell-path of academe. Despite it all, and like Dante looking up in the final tercet of each of the three books in his *Commedia* to see again the stars each time, Howard looked up that last, narrow, dark flight of stairs, and, eyes brightening, was yet again drawn to the work in his library chambers that day.)

Even as Edna regularly longed to appropriate the words of her other husband, then, such devotional reading habits of hers nonetheless were regularly interrupted by the scholarly work she shared with Howard. It was work that both Howard and Edna knew would help make the genius and wisdom of the other husband available to readers everywhere. According to St. Olaf colleague William Narum, however, Edna "more than once cried out about what this man Kierkegaard has done to her life, forcing her to spend hours chasing down the exact meaning of some word or phrase he used."

Still, Edna distanced herself from the academic world into which she married—and not only so as not, in her words, to *go mad*. She also knew to practice Christian devotional reading as daily invitations that correspond with daily deeds, for that practice was grounded less in scholarly abstraction and more in day-to-day concrete living in the truth one understands. At the outset of one lecture she presented, she suggested that she had no use for "footnotes, cross-references, and all that scholarly paraphernalia." In another lecture, she was more lyrical:

> I am not a scholar. I do not drag behind me a freight train of footnotes but carry a backpack only enough to support what I say. Nor am I a theologian, not even an untrained theologian. I am merely someone who apparently was born with an infatuation for buttons, or buttoning Truths with a big letter "T" to life with a small letter "l"—namely, to provide what the Germans so aptly call [*Anknüpfungspunke*], buttoning up points, for the sacrament of the altar.

Such sentiments serve as preliminary insights by Edna to understand the Devotional Edna and, in the end, Edna reading Kierkegaard devotionally. For it was everywhere and often that Kierkegaard wrote how the scholarly, the intellect, and the sagacious are more often than not in conflict with concrete works of love prompted by an unencumbered devotional heart. Kierkegaard's Johannes Climacus puts it this way: "One person is good, another is sagacious, or the same person acts as good at one time, as sagacious at another, but simultaneously to see in the same thing what is most sagacious and to see it only in order to will the good is certainly difficult"— while Kierkegaard himself puts it similarly: "The sagacious person needs to take a lot of time and trouble to understand what the simple person at the joyous prompting of a pious heart feels no need to understand in lengthy detail, because he at once simply understands only the good." All of which is perhaps why Edna not only took genuine joy in translating the wisdom of Kierkegaard with Howard, but also why she regularly read Kierkegaard devotionally. So much of Kierkegaard's wisdom, in other words, nurtured Edna's own devotional proclivities, which in turn rendered her devotional relationship to the words of her other husband a testament to that Arabian proverb, *A fig tree, looking on a fig tree, becometh fruitful.*

Kierkegaard's many words critiquing the tedious ways of scholarship, however, did little to exempt him from being the object of Edna's pity as well. Edna reading Kierkegaard devotionally, in other words, did not mean that she turned a blind eye to Kierkegaard's shortcomings and personal prejudices. The opening of a chapter to her book *The Gayety of Grace* makes some of her complaints clear. (Entitled "Enter Søren Kierkegaard," this chapter of hers imaginatively constructs a conversation between him and a composite of six "selves" that collectively make up Edna's corporate self*):

> SØREN KIERKEGAARD: Too many women! I hate babbling, gabbling women!
>
> *(Whereupon my six Me's promptly nucleate and I stand there a Corporate Me, an I, alone with him.... Our eyes meet and take each other's soundings.)*

---

*Edna's identified "selves," which converse back and forth with each other throughout the book, include *Me-R* (her respectable, establishment self), *Me-I* (who "represents everything that starts with *imp*—impulsive, impertinent, impudent, impetuous, improvident—and often impenitent"), *Me-T* (who "does not know if she is a Philosopher or a Theologian but actually is neither"), *Me-N* (who is "an amateur Naturalist and ardent Nature lover and is *anti*-but-not-necessarily-*un*-intellectual"), *Me-E* (who is "an Ecstatic, dancing in solitude to Bach and Vivaldi"), *Me-D* (who is her Despair—which later transforms into *Me-Hope*), while *I* is the *Corporate Edna*, which may only be "a mask for one or all of the others, a protective front when one or all of them feels threatened."

I: You were full of contrasting selves, too, you know, only you called them pseudonyms, and you situated your true self somewhere between your antitheses, Johannes Climacus and Anti-Climacus, but I suspect that the man Søren Kierkegaard filled the whole space between them, and even that space was not enough.

S.K. *(a chuckling infectious laugh shaking his whole body)*: You have been spying on me!

I: As you spied on everybody! Oh, you played many roles—Kierkegaard the spy, Kierkegaard the gadfly, Kierkegaard the whip. You made a whip of men's pleasant vices and scourged them unmercifully.

S.K.: Which one did you summon when you summoned me here?

I: Kierkegaard, the teacher and preacher of the Grace of God.

S.K. *(genuinely startled)*: I have not often been labelled so graciously!

I: The Hymn to Grace is pretty hard to find in, with, and under the lampooning of men.

A few pages later, Edna spars again with the misogynist in Kierkegaard:

S.K.: ... For a woman you—

I: None of your deprecatory remarks about women, please! It is not tolerated today. Nor should it be! It really was inexcusable of you, Sir!

S.K.: Like a woman you change the subject.

I: *You* did! You inserted the subject of women.

A few more pages later, Edna chides Kierkegaard for his general critique of his religious forebear, Martin Luther (the latter of whom has recently entered into Edna's imaginative conversation): "*Tie stille! (Kierkegaard is amazed to be told to shut up in his own language.)* Quit blaming Luther for what the generations after him did to politicize, secularize, and nullify his principle of Grace!"*

---

*Forty-seven years later, Clare Carlisle, in her 2019 biography of Kierkegaard, echoes Edna's simultaneous critique of and praise for Kierkegaard:

> While living in uncomfortably close proximity to Kierkegaard, I have sometime found myself disliking him—a painful feeling, similar to the pain of finding fault with a loved one. His books give his readers high expectations; his lyrical religious discourses describe exquisite ideals, like how a pure human heart reflects God's goodness as truly as a calm, still sea reflects the heavens. Yet in his journals he rehearsed his petty fixations, his jealousy of his rivals' success, his bitter fury at those who slighted him, his debilitating pride. He often felt sorry for himself, justified himself, blamed others for his disappointments. Does this make him a hypocrite who preached something

As a further look below at Edna reading Kierkegaard devotionally suggests, she could not give up on Søren for the prejudicial logs in his eye just as much as she could not give up on Howard for his penchant for footnotes. She loved her two men both not only despite, but also because of the logs and the footnotes. Perhaps this aspect of Edna's generosity might have existed because Edna, more than either Howard or Søren, could more easily and effortlessly remove herself from academic, scholarly, and intellectual worlds dominated by abstraction—existing, as it were, in those worlds without being of those worlds. She did this, I suspect, to attune herself more properly to things like baking bread to feed any and all who crossed the threshold of the home she made with Howard; or to reveal to anyone within her

---

he did not practice or experience? On the contrary: Kierkegaard's remarkable ability to invoke the goodness, purity and peace for which he longed was inseparable from the storms that raged and twisted in his soul—connected by precisely this longing for what he knew he lacked. His philosophy is well known for its paradoxes, and Kierkegaard's restless desire for rest, peace, stillness, was a paradox—and a truth—that he lived daily. And like every human being, his life was a mixture of elements both petty and profound, which could exert equally powerful claims upon him.

physical orbit a more expressive and graceful gayety in all things great and small with which she regularly came into contact; or to be ever-attentive to the needs, joys, and sufferings of people who crossed her path daily. She felt perfectly comfortable living with and loving a cigar-smoking scholar-translator-husband and her other cigar-smoking scholar-author-husband without being subsumed by the toxic odor that scholarship in the abstract often exudes. Her more intimate and less meticulous brand of scholarly life supported, informed, and accented her daily life more than it controlled or dominated that daily life. Like the practice of daily devotional reading itself, whatever words she more casually but no less earnestly read each day from books were words that simply set the tone for how she acted and the correspondent deeds that she enacted that day.

❧

If Kierkegaard's authorship offers readers a sustained devotional reflection informing correspondent ethical action, such a devotional practice begins not with reading devotionally the books of Søren Kierkegaard but with remembering one's creator in the days of one's youth. Kierkegaard describes this kind of remembering as "youth's best thought," a "rosebud" that "does not wither," which is the very presupposition embedded in Christ's injunction that "unless you turn around and become like children you will never enter the kingdom of heaven." In the dedication to her religiously oriented children's book *Clues to the Kingdom* (addressed to her "garland of grandchildren"), Edna Hong describes this early childhood remembering as "the ordinary happiness of the Kingdom of the First Spontaneity." Such remembrance doesn't end in the days of a person's developmental youth. Rather, the remembrance may prompt a person to become like a child again and again as one matures by simply remembering through devotion what it means to be a human being, or what Kierkegaard calls "assimilating" in mature years "childhood transfigured." Remembering thus takes joy in "the extra-ordinary happiness of the Kingdom of the Second Spontaneity." Just as a child who inhabits the Kingdom of the First Spontaneity obediently finds meaning in make-believe stories, the meaning-making devotional reader who inhabits the Kingdom of the Second Spontaneity becomes the deliberate practitioner of what Frances Maughan-Brown above calls "obedient reading, one that *believes* the text." By doing so, the devotional reader follows Christ's advice to *turn around*.

Edna writes about this ever-recurrent Second Spontaneity in an autobiography of her Wisconsin childhood in this way: "When all is said and done, this is perhaps why I am most deeply grateful to the living institution of the church and will hang with it: it is the only institution I know which has the

principle of and the power for ever-recurrent renewal." (Edna's use of the idiom *hang with* has a hip-
sterish lilt these days that would be foreign to Edna
writing in 1974—even as its contemporary meaning
is not entirely incongruous with hers. Here, Edna
treats the verb "to hang" in its literal denotation of
*being suspended by or alongside of to the point of being
crucified with*. This speculation echoes Kierkegaard's
essential meaning behind his epigram to his *Philosophical Fragments* from Shakespeare's *Twelfth
Night*, "Better well hanged than ill wed" (1.5.20-21),
that is, better to be hung or crucified with Christ, as
Johannes Climacus notes, than "brought into sys-
tematic in-law relationship with the whole world.")

As for her First Spontaneity (remembering her
creator in her actual childhood), Edna notes that "at
the tender age of three I had already fallen in love
with the church, and I have never fallen out of love
with it." By suggesting above that she will for better
or for worse continue to commit herself to (that is,
to *hang with*) the church, Edna also suggests not only
that the church was not perfect, but that its imper-
fections did not alter her devotion to it and its central mission. "Pathetic preachers, bad interpreters of
good doctrine, fanatic fundamentalists and fanatic
disgruntalists—none has disaffected me in my love
affair with the church. Somehow grace seemed always able to press in on my small soul in spite of
myself and those humans who with the best of

intentions plug all the ingresses of the soul." Her commentary comes as much from the standpoint of a mature and reflective congregant as from channeling Kierkegaard, who writes similarly about how it is possible to be a good reader of the church's message while covering up the multitude of sins of its earthly (ad)ministrations:

> My listener, even if the appointed [religious] guide in the place where you live were incompetent, well, if you so choose, be the good listener who still benefits from his mediocre [religious] discourse. And if the person speaking here is perhaps too young or perhaps expresses himself unclearly or his thought is unclear— well, my listener, then put the discourse aside or, if you choose, do the great thing, be the good reader who benefits even from an inadequate discourse. As a matter of fact, just as there is supposed to be a power of discourse that can almost work miracles, so there is also a listener's power that can work miracles if the listener so chooses. He says, "I want to be built up," and so he is built up.

Remembering good reading habits in the days of Edna's youth, then, complimented how she thought and remembered her creator daily. Being a good reader was also essential to appropriating words devotionally. "We arranged and re-arranged the furniture to play school, church, house," Edna writes, "or we shut the door of our room and remained alone with a book. For that habit, too, the habit of reading, we got from mother, for she insisted on 'peace and quiet' in the evening so that she could assimilate every printed word in *The Lutheran Herald, The Prairie Farmer, The Wisconsin Agriculturist, The Taylor County Star-News*—and always and always her favorite devotional book, *Streams in the Desert.* After darkness fell, there were but two alternatives for us children in a country home without electricity—to join the readers around the hissing Coleman lamp—or go to bed. No wonder we became readers who read every morsel of print we could lay our hands on, be it good, bad, or indifferent." (In addition to these devotional reading habits of Edna's comporting with what Kierkegaard writes above, her habits are also reflected by what Kierkegaard's Quidam writes in *Stages on Life's Way* about reading even the most mediocre of text with passion: "The less one has, the more one sees. Take a book, the poorest one written, but read it with the passion that it is the only book you will read—ultimately you will read everything out of it, that is, as much as there was in yourself, and you could never get more out of reading, even if you read the best of books." —Such is how I remember Edna reading...almost everything.)

As Edna Hong's obituary attests, early reading also included devotional literature spawned by her churchgoing. She "grew up in Our Savior's Lutheran

Church, three and a half miles from the Hatlestad farm. Our Savior's formed her: she later wrote that here was where she learned by heart Luther's *Small Catechism* and Pontoppidan's *Explanation of Luther's Small Catechism*." The 1529 and 1737 devotional works of Martin Luther and Danish author and Lutheran bishop of the Church of Norway Erik Pontoppidan were perhaps the first two pieces of literature that Edna read devotionally. In this context, the devotional practice was not only a daily practice, but also a way in which she was fully able to appropriate the text less by "brain" (rote) and more by "heart" (the latter expression being what George Steiner considers both "vital" and "the most important tribute any human being can pay" to a text in particular and literacy in general). Such practice prompts the child of the First Spontaneity to grow into the matured "child" of the Second Spontaneity, or one who is capable of reduplicating the truth of the text in her daily life. As Kierkegaard notes: "The more mature person learns in another way. If someone were to memorize the Bible, there could be something beautiful inasmuch as there was something childlike in his behavior, but essentially the adult learns only by appropriating, and he essentially appropriates the essential by doing it."

Edna's childhood devotional reading and upbringing—remembering her creator in the days of her youth—also befits the devotional practice of a favorite fictional character of hers, Father Zosima in Dostoevsky's *The Brothers Karamazov*. In her remarkable book, The Brothers Karamazov *and the Poetics of Memory*, Diane Oenning Thompson writes of this practice:

> Zosima makes the whole world his own ("love every blade of grass") because it all arouses the memory of the Word which he took into his consciousness as a child. Zosima lives in continuous conversation with the Word and he reads the world by it. Everything partakes in a double level of signification, the sacred and the earthly. His whole consciousness is so filled by his memory of the Word, that for him, memory, the Word and consciousness have completely merged and become one and the same.

How Edna and Zosima judge the value of childhood ultimately agrees with Kierkegaard's opinion on the matter: "*What judgment do you make on your childhood and youth?* Do you judge that it was foolishness and fancies? Or do you judge that you were at the time closest to the Most High? Just tell me how you judge your childhood and your youth, and I will tell you who you are."

This intensive childlike consciousness of Edna's is arguably what fully manifested the Devotional Edna in ways revealed to all who came within her orbit. "When she wasn't reading or writing," one obituary writer noted, Edna "enjoyed baking whole-wheat bread and going on walks with the children. She liked spending time outdoors at the couple's cabin in Hovland, Minnesota, and loved to explore the natural world. 'She kept that playfulness, that childhood joy, all her life,' niece Kay Hong said. 'There was an openness to her that was like a full, loving heart.'" Daughter Mary Hong Loe writes that her mother "once told me that her greatest wish for her children was that we'd have rich inner lives, vivid imaginations. For her, this wellspring from within was the essence of her being."* When an interviewer once asked Edna if she had any specific principle to which she adhered when translating Kierkegaard, she harkened back to her childhood and to how she played with words: "Well, if I have [any specific principles], they are very unconscious. I'm not a

---

*A quintessential depiction of a child having a rich inner life—and one that may have helped spawn Edna's wish for her children—is from Kierkegaard when he has his pseudonym Johannes Climacus recall the times his father would help him get to know the sites and scenes of Copenhagen without ever leaving the confines of their home. Instead, the father would usher the son through their home and prompt the son to imagine people and places and conversations that existed outside the walls. Surely such imaginary exercises helped Johannes Climacus and Kierkegaard himself depict their respective external and internal worlds throughout their literary lives, lives that were composed chiefly from within the walls of their own homes.

principled person [chuckling]. I just *dive in*; it's the task, and one just dives in and does it. Then, of course, I love words. Ever since I was nine years old I wrote stories. I love words, I love to *play* with words; and translating is a creative sort of thing." In her eulogy on the occasion of Edna Hong's death, Pamela Schwandt pinpoints this Archimedean point of Edna's devotional self: "Above all, Edna was childlike, but not the least bit childish. She was mature in her Christian life, and therefore free to become as simple as a child in her faith. Oliver Wendell Holmes, Jr., said, 'I wouldn't give a fig for simplicity this side of complexity, but I'd give my life for simplicity on the far side of complexity.' Edna had reached the simplicity on that far side of complexity." —Which is not to say that Edna was a St. Francis-like—or, more fittingly, St. Clare-like— saint, nor would Edna ever think of herself as such. Pamela Schwandt adds: "Edna was not naturally pure of heart. She was a sinner, like all the rest of us. Resentment, jealousy, hurtful words spoken in anger, wrongful desire, self-deception—these were Edna's sins, as surely as they are ours. They are garden variety sins, noxious little weeds that are mighty enough to destroy inner peace for a lifetime. Edna the Sinner's heart was not naturally pure. It needed to be made pure. And this she knew well."

CR

Sin-consciousness is located at the center of Kierke-gaard's philosophical and religious anthropology. It was also at the center of Edna's life, for sin-consciousness is God-consciousness in its humble, contrite, repentant, confessional acknowledgement of needing God. Sin-consciousness twines together the incommensurate categories of the temporal and the eternal to their tightest torque. As Lillian and David Swenson write: "When the religious man becomes religiously aware of the eternal and the life of the eternal, it arouses in him a sense of his own moral imperfection, and gives a new significance to the moral task because it determines that task as the reconstruction of the individual man and his mode of life." Edna reading Kierkegaard devotionally, her response to such literature, and her own contribution to devotional literature all reveal her own sense of sin-consciousness, with its residual and alternating attention to suffering and optimism, or what Victor Frankl calls *tragic optimism.*

In imaginative dialogue with Kierkegaard in her book *The Gayety of Grace,* Edna Hong begins to render clearly and concretely what Kierkegaard thinks and, by extension, what she thinks about sin-consciousness, beginning with particularizing and thereby personalizing sin-consciousness. Such particularization in turn speaks to how only by sin-consciousness does a person come to need God and thereby come to God—something for which earnest, inward, individually-oriented devotional literature also aims:

> S.K. [speaking to Edna]: It is easy, almost cozy, to confess total, universal, collective guilt. The painful thing is to change a generality into a particularity. The agony is to change people into eaches, to introduce the "I", to switch from "they" or "we" to "I".... The anguished conscience! It is a painful road to travel from the general to the particular, from the impersonal to the person, from "they" and "we" to "I"....
>
> I: Of course, if it ends in Grace.
>
> S.K. *(sharply)*: Madame, it is Grace all the way! The consciousness of sin, the anguished conscience, is not the gate to Grace, it *is* the Grace of God. No one who approached God from any other standpoint than that of his own moral imperfection will ever know the height and the breadth and the depth of God's love.... Remove the anguished conscience and you may as well lock the churches and convert them into dance halls....
>
> I: ...But—and here is the nub of the matter— *do we always need to be watching the movements of the inner being?* ... All this constant self-scrutinizing leads to an anguished conscience, but do we want that, do we need that? Doesn't the anguished conscience end in despair...?
>
> ...

S.K.: I agree, I agree, and didn't I say it many times? There is nothing more dangerous, more paralyzing than a certain isolating self-scrutiny where one sits and constantly stares at his own navel, and one's whole life, all one's relationships, become infected with self, poisoned by self. But this is not true at all of the self-scrutiny before God, where one discovers that even his human pluperfectness is imperfect. Anguished conscience before God, yes—provisional and partial—but it is not a shameful secret, a humiliating embarrassment. Indeed, to the contrary, it becomes a kind of joke between you and God. You make no bones about it. You admit it, you make a clean and honest admission. You need God, and you need Grace.... Indeed, Madame, I wrote a discourse on this and entitled it "Man's Perfection Is His Need of God." God's judgment upon you is a good and perfect gift. How else would you know that you had hurt or failed love? Your despair is a good and perfect gift. It teaches you not only to take refuge in Grace but also how to live in Grace, make use of Grace. It leads you to Alleluia.... Grace, you see, is never a substitute for the anguished conscience, for repentance. Self-knowledge of one's nothingness created the condition which allows God to dwell in you. The joke is that one can boast without blushing, as Paul did. To speak of God's grace is to speak indirectly of one's own nothingness, unworthiness. The joke is that

one's nothingness is one's greatness. And you
are afraid that the anguished conscience leads
to a perpetual paralysis of despair! Oh, Madame, it leads to saints, for what are saints but
weak things filled with the boundless grace of
God!

So, what is the rub for readers when Edna's imaginative conversation with Søren unpacks such central problems of existence so effortlessly? Where sin-
consciousness and the religious language that is used
to discuss it is directly invoked, as Edna does
above—*that* is also where so many secular readers in
Huxleyan brave new church-turned-dance hall
worlds quickly lose interest, bow out, or (what Kierkegaard often predicted) take offense—all by the
very talk of religion. In Edna's 1989 book *Box 66,
Sumac Lane: A Lively Correspondence on Sin and
Sanctity*, Editor Tate Kuhlman says as much in his
rejection letter to Molly Mortenson. Although he
notes that her manuscript on sanctification has
much merit, "our market researchers are convinced
that the book will not sell. The subject matter has
little appeal today. Sanctification does not seem to
be an aspiration of the present generation. Regretta-
bly, the modern mind finds the dogma somewhat
antiquated. Moreover, the word 'saint' has become
more or less meaningless in the modern world." Similarly, Kuhlman's secretary, Martha Hoffman, writes
to Molly, noting that "the only sin today is to think

anything a sin. You never hear anyone preach about the seven deadly sins anymore." What's the point, then, of reading sacred or devotional literature if the kind of longing that Edna called "man's umbilical cord to the eternal" actually *has* dried up and dissolved from disuse? For Edna, the real point was that she could never make herself come to believe that the absence of the eternal in one's self was even possible in a human being. She could say, along with Kierkegaard, that "it seems to me that something higher is constantly moving within me; I believe that I cannot justify anything else but continuing to serve it as long as possible."

And so Edna repeatedly imagined, chose, and willed to be informed by and devoted to what she called a healthy sense of guilt that she knew coursed through her blood, grateful for having appropriated the concept of sin-consciousness and the vocabulary of religious language at such an early age, to which she thanks the church

> for placing the idea of *ought* into me. True, the *ought* and the *nots* were taught me first, they sometimes were shallow and superficial *ought nots*.... But under the tutelage of the Word and the Spirit, the *ought* manifested itself until I could see that often the very goodness of the "good people," myself included, was selfish self-interest and disobedience to God's *ought*. In short, I learned.... a concept of healthy guilt and a conviction that there is no place for

> vanity in me.... because guilt is the only way I
> have to know when I have hurt someone I love.

Such admission of guilt, as Kierkegaard's Johannes Climacus maintains, is the "expression for the strongest self-assertion of existence," an unambiguous being-inspired *I am* (guilty) as opposed to a patently nihilistic *I am not* (guilty). Guilt becomes evidence that a person is endowed with both freedom and the ethical responsibility for how that freedom ought to be wielded, a responsibility that Edna in her own understanding of Kierkegaardian self-honesty never gainsaid.

Edna's sense of guilt is subsequently related to what Edna calls "self-seeing" in her book *The Downward Ascent,* evident in the opening line of the book's first chapter: "My ardent and joyful faith, the *Hallelujah* that sings within me, and my disgust and distrust of myself, my unlovely self, are both truths about me." Understanding these binary truths in tandem indicates to her that to choose the good is the only ethical option: "*either* I can and may sink to the lowest low of my fallen nature (which is not to sink to the beast but *below* the beast, for the opposite of the divine is not the bestial but the demonic), *or* I can and may rise to the heights of my other, my divine nature, my noble birthright, my created-in-the-image-of-God birthright." —All of which confirms something that Kierkegaard claims regarding classic devotional literature: "Here, as everywhere, is what the old devotional books* explain so profoundly, so experientially, so instructively. They teach that God sometimes lets the believer stumble and fall in some temptation or other, precisely in order to humble him and thereby to establish him better in the good."

ભ

Built upon her own sin-consciousness, Edna Hong dedicated herself to neighbor love. Hers was a task that regularly affirmed Kierkegaard's devotional prompts, which asked her if she was "now living in such a way that you are aware of being a single individual and thereby aware of your eternal responsibility before God; are you living in such a way that this awareness can acquire the time and stillness and liberty of action to penetrate your life relationships? You are not asked to withdraw from life, from an honorable occupation, from a happy domestic life— on the contrary, that awareness will support and transfigure and illuminate your conduct in the relationships of your life."***

---

*In his translation of *The Sickness unto Death*, Bruce Kirmmse notes three devotional authors to whom Kierkegaard was presumably referring here, including Johannes Tauler (1300–1361), Thomas à Kempis (1380–1471), and Johannes Arndt (1555–1621).
**I thank Sergia Hay for reminding me of this passage, for it befits Edna Hong's adult life. I also thank Hay for her own

As for any religiously oriented person called to such a task, the work begins in the psychical wilderness of sustained solitude and reflection. Edna, Howard, and daughter Mary collectively wrote about this in a book that explores growing up in Minnesota:

> Only in the gift of time and space and in the experience of aloneness can the human spirit become attentive to its potentiality and

---

discussion of the same passage in her book, *Ethical Silence*, for it, too, suits Edna. Hay (who acknowledges Edna at the outset of her book as a mentor) focuses on Kierkegaard's first and second ethics as introduced by his pseudonym Vigilius Haufniensis in *The Concept of Anxiety*. The second ethics—Kierkegaard's Christian ethics—presupposes sin and grace and, according to Hay, "originates in actuality and is justified by faith." "In contrast to language's outwardness," Hay writes later, "the second ethics is essentially inward. The second ethics' subject is the actual rather than the conceptual." Then, in her own discussion of the passage above from *Upbuilding Discourses in Various Spirits*, Hay writes that "through inwardness, one matures religiously, and also ethically…. Understood as the condition for religious and ethical maturity, inwardness does not indicate total absence of language nor the end of associations with others. Instead, Kierkegaard views inwardness as the foundation for authentic speech and action." —All of which speak to Edna Hong as an exemplar and practitioner of the second ethics as well as a person who read Kierkegaard devotionally and subsequently dedicated herself to the kind of neighbor love and the good of which Kierkegaard spoke.

relations, for attention is the power of the human spirit to be present to spirit—to oneself, to the spirit in whom we live, move, and have our being, to the spirit in another person, to the spirit in all that which we in our arrogated superiority call subhuman in creatures and creation. Solitude is needed for the green-growing of spirit and for the power of spirit to meet spirit with attention. Growing up in Minnesota provided us with solitude in good measure.

Edna's solitude was, in other words, essential preparation to meet the neighbor in ways that nourish the neighbor every day, from working to help settle displaced persons, war refugees, and prisoners of war for several years with the Lutheran World Federation after WWII to decades-long hospitality to anyone who crossed the threshold of the Hong house in Northfield, Minnesota. In one lecture of hers, Edna cites her national and religious influences in this matter:

> The Danes have a special pennant that they run up their flag poles to announce that the family is in residence and welcomes guests. The bright streamer announces, "we are at home." At the Lord's Supper in the upper room, so it seems to me, Jesus Christ ran up the blood-red, wine-purple flag of hospitality. "In this bread and in this wine," he said, "I shall ever be at home to you as often as you

partake of it...." He calls us to the vocation of hospitality, to give of ourselves as we have been given, make hospitality a habit of being. He calls us to fly the banner of hospitality at our homes every day, to make self-giving a daily experience. Just as he is present in the Eucharist, he calls us to be present to all others, to *all*, regardless of all human distinctions.

In a book he wrote about the Hongs and the Kierkegaard Library, Jack Schwandt offers a summary of testimonials citing Edna's daily acts of hospitality that she performed over the years:

> The citations that accompany [the Hongs' many] awards and degrees often point to the life of the Hongs, as well as to their work. One citation of Edna Hong observes that "she is a doer of good deeds," one who has, in the midst of raising a family of eight children, translating, writing, and speaking, always has been hospitable "to those in need, whether...a distracted St. Olaf student...or a distracted matron.... Some of the needy have required an evening of care, but some have required months, years of Edna Hong's time and energy, and she has given it freely." Another citation notes that "wherever they have lived [they] have always opened their doors to people—young and old—students, teachers, and internationally known scholars." This steady practice "has made them as well loved as they are respected." Their house, a third citation

states, has been "open...to an astonishing collection of...wayfarers. No one has counted
those who have eaten at their board, stayed
there for a night, or lived with them for years
on end. The basket that could gather the
crumbs from that table has not yet been woven."

This kind of hospitality for which Edna was
widely known translated to lives of characters in her
books as well. In her *Bright Valley of Love*, Edna portrays the concrete act of hospitable *being* as the fruits
of devotion. Having supper with one group of male
residents at the German charitable institute where
she worked, Frau Julia

had brought a huge [B]undt cake full of dried
currants from her own currant bush. She went
around the table serving a piece to each man,
her motherly face bright with her spontaneous,
childlike love. For her, time was now. The past
was past, all shiny and forgiven. The future
had been given into God's hands. Now was always right now, this unique moment when she
could share God's love—and she rejoiced in it.
Gunther watched her proudly, felt a glimmer
of brightening in the...men's mood. In her
presence they truly felt the reality of another
world than this dark, suffering world. But the
wonderful thing about Frau Julia was that she
herself, rooted in another world, did not feel

that she was being other-worldly in this world.
She just was!

So, too, Edna Hong: rooted in another world yet not other-worldly, she just *was*, living in the truth that she understood as she regularly responded devotionally to Kierkegaard's own call when he writes that "what I need is a person who does not gesticulate with his arms up in a pulpit or with his fingers upon a podium, but a person who gesticulates with his entire personal existence, with the willingness in every danger to will to express in action precisely what he teaches."

Just as Kierkegaard writes that "everything Christian is a concretion" and that "Christianity is the existential, a character-task," so Edna appropriated these devotionally-oriented Kierkegaardian precepts as both gifts and tasks daily. Or, as Molly Mortenson (that last alter ego of Edna's in her last published book) writes to her editor:

> The existentialism Kierkegaard fathered is plain and simple sanctification. I am sure that the statement would horrify most philosophers and some theologians, but they won't ever know anyway, and you won't tell, will you?... When he says, "Our age has completely forgotten what it means to exist," he uses the word in its original Latin meaning—to stand forth. He means more than when we say "merely existing".... For him it means to exist in what one understands, to exist in the truth one

understands. For Kierkegaard, for Christians, Christ is the truth, and to exist in the truth is to exist in Christ, to follow Christ, to walk the Way. You know, of course, that the earliest Christians were called "followers of the Way".... Read him and let him speak for himself.

Inasmuch as Edna Hong reading Kierkegaard devotionally knows and talks *about* all things Kierkegaardian in her works—from the dialectics of sin and sanctity and faith to suffering and joy and grace and the church—Edna's concrete person and character exemplified a lived Kierkegaardian life, one that regularly and capably transfigured learning and knowing by heart into the heart's active doing and being.

Notes

Unless otherwise indicated, all quoted Kierkegaard passages are from either the Princeton University Press *Kierkegaard's Writings* series (1978-98), the Princeton University Press *Kierkegaard's Journals and Notebooks* series (2007-20), or the Indiana University Press *Søren Kierkegaard Journals and Papers* series (1967-78).

Page 1. "…he cannot explain."—Søren Kierkegaard's Anti-Climacus. *The Sickness unto Death*, 23.

Page 1. "…was to meet Friday."—Søren Kierkegaard's Johannes Climacus. *Concluding Unscientific Postscript*, 460.

Page 3. "…handed down from the fathers." *Concluding Unscientific Postscript*, [629-30].

Page 4. "…onto the public stage of active witness." *Religion and the Nineteenth-Century Crisis of Culture*, by George Pattison (Cambridge: Cambridge University Press, 2009), 238.

Page 4. …is not "strictly speaking…religious." *The Point of View*, 31.

Page 5. "…in much fear and trembling." *The Point of View*, 46.

Page 5. …in a journal entry, "is an epigram for the sake of awakening." *Kierkegaard's Journals and Notebooks* 4:319/VIII^1 A 549 (1848).

Page 5. … "an awareness of the holy." *Practice in Christianity*, 139.

Page 7. ...and Victor Eremita ("Victorious Hermit"). See *Kierkegaard, Pietism, and Holiness,* by Christopher B. Barnett (New York: Ashgate Publishing, 2011), 116.

Page 7. ...than does "edifying" and "devotional." *Eighteen Upbuilding Discourses,* 503.

Page 7. ...defense of the word "upbuilding" compelling. See *Eighteen Upbuilding Discourses,* 503-05.

Page 8. "...appropriation of ethical and religious truths." *Søren Kierkegaard's Journals and Papers* 4:759.

Page 8. ...assume the rank of devotionals. See *Without Authority,* "Historical Introduction."

Page 10. "...is propaedeutic to ethico-religious development." *Kierkegaard, Pietism, and Holiness,* 68, 77. The journal entry Barnett cites is *Søren Kierkegaard's Journals and Papers* 2:318/VII[1] A 587 (1848).

Page 10. ...whom he often affectionately calls "my reader." See, for example, *Eighteen Upbuilding Discourses,* xix-xxi, 5, 53, 107, 179, 231, 295.

Page 10. "...with monastic precision" to the reading of devotional books. *The Prayers of Kierkegaard,* ed. Perry D. LeFevre (Chicago: University of Chicago Press, 1956), 197.

Page 11. "...that 'only the one who was in anxiety finds rest.'" *Philosopher of the Heart: The Restless Life of Søren Kierkegaard,* by Clare Carlisle (New York: Farrar, Straus and Giroux, 2019), 170-71, 178. Carlisle quotes from *Kierkegaard's Eighteen Upbuilding Discourses,* 321, 324 and *Fear and Trembling,* tr. Sylvia Walsh (Cambridge: Cambridge University Press, 2006), 21.

Page 12. ..."really, how many...have the time, the ability, and the interest to read?" *Kierkegaard's Journals and Notebooks* 4:147/VIII¹ A 131 (1847).

Page 14. "...and this is very far indeed from Mynster's Christianity." *Kierkegaard in Golden Age Denmark*, by Bruce Kirmmse (Bloomington: Indiana University Press, 1990), 429.

Page 14. ...may a reader begin to live life forward. See *Early Polemical Writings*, 255 (n97).

Page 14. ...restlessness oriented toward inward deepening." *For Self-Examination*, 23, 24.

Page 14. ...—a restlessness that Kierkegaard equates with faith. See *For Self-Examination*, 17.

Page 15. "...to bear witness to the human condition." *Philosopher of the Heart*, xi.

Page 16. ...hundreds of references to God exist from Kierkegaard's earliest works to his latest. *Kierkegaard's Journals and Papers* 2:566.

Page 16. "...but of devotion to God." *The Point of View*, 74, 73.

Pages 17-21. Testimonials from Contemporaries of Kierkegaard. *Kierkegaard: Letters and Documents*, tr. Henrik Rosenmeier (Princeton: Princeton University Press, 1978), 381, 382-83, 384, 379, 380, 401, 403, 404, 387.

Page 24. "old, short little books that lead to a holy life." See *Kierkegaard, Pietism and Holiness*, 80. Barnett's source for Arndt's words is Christian Braw's *Bücher im Staube: Die Theologie Johann Arndts in ihrem Verhältnis zur Mystik* (Leiden, 1985), 43.

Page 29. **Reading, a colleague of mine always reminded me, is rocket science.** Thanks to Susan Richardson of Red Wing, Minnesota for this.

Page 29. **"...as Henry David Thoreau knew that books..."** See *Walden*, by Henry David Thoreau, ed. Walter Harding (New York: Houghton Mifflin Co., 1995), 98 (from "Reading").

Page 30. **"...into the safer realm of objective narrative."** *Something About Kierkegaard*, by David Swenson (Minneapolis: Augsburg Publishing House, 1941 and 1945), 2.

Page 31. **"...and grateful for the opportunity to write about him."** *Kierkegaard,* Julia Watkin (London: Continuum, 1997), ix-x.

Page 31. **"...I find him as rich and profound as ever."** *Kierkegaard and Spirituality, by* C. Stephen Evans (Grand Rapids, MI: Eerdmans Publishing Company, 2019), viii.

Page 31. **"...and with little trace of dogmatism or moralism."** *Philosopher of the Heart*, 261.

Page 32. **"...this truth concerning their own eternal happiness."** *Concluding Unscientific Postscript*, 21.

Page 33. **"...a good home"...transforming them into something of great worth.** See *Eighteen Upbuilding Discourses*, 107.

Page 33m. **...one of his eighteen upbuilding discourses "To Need God is a Human Being's Highest Perfection."** *Eighteen Upbuilding Discourses*, 297-326.

Page 33n. **..."perhaps the most profound" of the 18 discourses.** *Lectures on the Religious Thought of Søren Kierkegaard*, by Eduard Geismar (Minneapolis: Augsburg Publishing House, 1937), 65.

Page 34. …made them "needful of comfort." See *Eighteen Upbuilding Discourses*, 303.

Page 34. …as Kierkegaard also suggests, "that basically it is shut out." See *Eighteen Upbuilding Discourses*, 301.

Page 34. …of that person "having a deeply religious need." See the two opening epigraphs to this book.

Page 35. "…goes through life without discovering that he needs God." *Eighteen Upbuilding Discourses*, 303.

Page 35. …*religious need* or *old devotional books* or *spiritual trial* that Johannes Climacus uses. See second epigraph to this book.

Page 35. "…such an inspired character would remind it of what has been forgotten?" *Fear and Trembling*, 101-02.

Page 36. "…also forgotten what it means to exist humanly." *Concluding Unscientific Postscript*, 249.

Page 36. …"obedient reading, one that *believes* the text." *The Lily's Tongue: Figure and Authority in Kierkegaard's Lily Discourses*, by Frances Maughan-Brown (Albany: State University of New York Press, 2019), 155.

Page 38. "…the response to the absolute expression of the absolute relation." *Concluding Unscientific Postscript*, 459.

Page 39. …how Kierkegaard defines Christianity's essence. See *Søren Kierkegaard's Journals and Papers* 1:434/X^4 A 734 (1851).

Page 39. …upon the sea like Kierkegaard's king-fisher. See *Without Authority*, 7; *Søren Kierkegaard's Journals and Notebooks* 2:78/II A 612 (1837).

Page 39. "…in all eternity become more for the person

who comes later." *Philosophical Fragments*, 104.

Page 39. "...in order then either to be offended or to believe." *Practice in Christianity*, 105.

Page 40. ..."step out onto the public stage of active witness." See p. 4.

Page 40. ...how love builds up. See, for example, *Works of Love*, 216-17.

Page 40. "...disperses the fogs of busy care." *Eighteen Upbuilding Discourses*, 248-49.

Page 41. "...the limited plans for your life and its future...." *Without Authority*, 18–19.

Page 43. "...lying unfurled next to the original." *Taking Kierkegaard Personally: First Person Responses*, eds. Jamie Lorentzen and Gordon Marino (Macon, GA: Mercer University Press, 2020), 292.

Page 44. ...by becoming "less of one." *Taking Kierkegaard Personally*, 32.

Page 44. "...*Pereat* the commentators! [Let them die!]" *Kierkegaard's Journals and Notebooks* 7:154/X^2 A 556, 555 (1850).

Page 44. ...am always in the wrong. See *Either/Or* II, 339ff.

Page 45. ..."become more and more pronounced." *Eighteen Upbuilding Discourses*, 165.

Page 46. ...in the inwardness of appropriation. See *Upbuilding Discourses in Various Spirits*, 5.

Page 46. "...self-evident thoughts should come so late to our minds." *The Brothers Karamazov*, by Fyodor

Dostoevsky, trs. Richard Pevear and Larissa Volokhonsky (London: Quartet Books, 1990), 317.

Page 47. "...It just takes me a while to realize things." From *Rough and Rowdy Ways*, by Bob Dylan (New York: Columbia Records, 2020).

Page 46n. "A Reading Lesson." *Taking Kierkegaard Personally*, 294.

Page 47. ".... This is the crisis and is entirely in order." *Stages on Life's Way*, 152-53.

Page 53. "...he drew you in, but also brought you to a halt." *Philosopher of the Heart*, 83.

Page 53. ...and a whole book section on the verse in another. See *Christian Discourses*, 262-67 and *Practice in Christianity*, 11-68, respectively.

Page 53. "At the altar the Savior opens his arms." *Without Authority*, 184.

Page 54. "...at the edge of what humans know." *My Bright Abyss: Meditation of a Modern Believer*, by Christian Wiman (New York: Farrar, Straus, and Giroux, 2013), 57, 81.

Page 54. ...that commences "as in the ethical." *Kierkegaard's Journals and Notebooks* 11.2:104/Paper 366:3 (1847).

Page 56. ...(as Kierkegaard's Johannes Climacus suggests.) See *57 Fragments*, 104. See also p. 39 above.

Page 57. ...that Christianity brought sensuality into the world. See *Either/Or* I, 61.

Page 59. "...absolutely consistent expression of what is

purely godly." *Kierkegaard's Journals and Notebooks* 4:215/VIII[1] A 81 (1847).

Page 61. **"...all his energies were devoted to that endeavor."** *Receiving Søren Kierkegaard: The Early Impact and Transmission of His Thought*, by Habib C. Malik (Washington, D.C.: The Catholic University of America Press, 1997), 57-58.

Page 61. ***Think about your Creator in the days of your youth.*** Ecclesiastes 12:1.

Page 61. **..."be content with thinking about your Creator."** *Eighteen Upbuilding Discourses*, 246, 235.

Page 61. **...to "exist in the truth one understands."** See *Søren Kierkegaard's Journals and Papers* 2:537/IX A 438 (1848); cf. *Practice in Christianity*, 134.

Page 62. **"...because I wish material for observation."** *Stages on Life's Way*, 463.

Page 62. ***...communication of a little religious knowledge.*** See p. 54.

Page 63. **...pseudonym H. H. writes, "then good night to Christianity."** *Without Authority*, 93.

Page 64. **...as ethically and religiously wounding "from behind."** See *Christian Discourses*, 161-246.

Page 64. **...a "devotional classic" beyond compare in the nineteenth century.** *Purity of Heart Is to Will One Thing*, by Søren Kierkegaard, tr. Douglas Steere (New York: Harper and Row, 1948), 25.

Page 64. **"...Kierkegaard does well to begin with it."** Quoted in translation in the "Historical Introduction" of *Upbuilding Discourses in Various Spirits*, xiv.

Page 66. …**does not mind being deceived.** See, e.g., *Upbuilding Discourses in Various Spirits*, 291.

Page 66n. "**…the hard existential work prior to confession.**" *Taking Kierkegaard Personally*, 205.

Page 67. "**…at the cost of much time and much grief.**" *Purity of Heart*, Steere tr., 54-55.

Page 67. "**…the discourse at any rate has understood him.**" *Eighteen Upbuilding Discourses*, 250.

Page 68. …**communication that he calls an "oughtness capability."** *Søren Kierkegaard's Journals and Papers* 1:281/VIII^2 B 83 (1847).

Page 68. …**"the boring categories of the good."** *The Point of View*, 92.

Page 68. …**of being "glad to the brink of fear."** *Emerson: Essays and Lectures* (New York: Library of America, 1981), 10.

Page 69. …**pounds "sand into every rat hole of self-deception."** *The Essential Kierkegaard*, ed. Howard and Edna Hong (Princeton: Princeton University Press, 2000), 269.

Page 69. …**ethical and ethical-religious truth.** See *The Concept of Irony*, 131, 327.

Page 69. "**…and look, one has entrapped oneself.**" *Kierkegaard's Journals and Notebooks* 6:290/X^2 A 93 (1849).

Page 70. …**"a synthesis and thus naturally, if you will, a born hypocrite."** *Kierkegaard's Journals and Notebooks* 9:84/X^4 A 638 (1852).

Page 71. …**was written "before the face of God."** See p. 64.

Page 71. ...he searched "for ways to stave off Kierke-gaard's demand." *Taking Kierkegaard Personally*, 206.

Page 71. ...to float out "on the depths of 70,000 fathoms of water." *Taking Kierkegaard Personally*, 313. Here, Bowen invokes Kierkegaard's "70,000 fathoms" motif, which may be found in *Stages on Life's Way*, 444-45, 470-71, 477; *Concluding Unscientific Postscript*, 140, 204, 232, 288; *Søren Kierkegaard's Journals and Papers* 5:275/VI B 18 (1844-45); and *Kierkegaard's Journals and Notebooks* 4:82/VII^1 A 221 (1847); 7:111/X^2 A 493 (1850); and 8:260/X^4 A 114 (1851).

Page 72. "...the idea you have had about my serving something true." *Late Writings*, 106.

Page 72. ...that they shouldn't so quickly believe every-thing they thought. See *For Self-Examination*, 44; cf. *Two Ages*, 10.

Page 72. "...except continuing to serve it as long as possi-ble." *Kierkegaard's Journals and Notebooks* 9:18/X^4 A 559 (1852). See also p. 121.

Page 72. "...prompt these to beat their wings." *Stages on Life's Way*, 657/VII^2 B 235 (1846-47); see also the wild goose parable in *Søren Kierkegaard's Journals and Papers* 3:389-90/XI^1 A 195 (1854).

Page 73. "...the Archimedean point...moves heaven and earth." *Kierkegaard's Journals and Notebooks* 4:108/VIII^1 A 60 (1847).

Page 74. "...the noise on earth makes it easy not to miss it." *Eighteen Upbuilding Discourses*, 243.

Page 74. ...before concluding that "this instant is the mo-ment of passion." *Concluding Unscientific Postscript*, 197.

Page 75. "…and the mountains slam." *Pilgrim at Tinker Creek*, by Annie Dillard (New York: HarperPerennial, 1985), 33, 34.

Page 75. "…but you can't come back all the way." From Bob Dylan's song, "Mississippi," on his 2001 *"Love and Theft"* CD.

Page 75. "…and one comes to it backward." *Without Authority*, 11.

Page 76. **Like Prospero at the end *The Tempest.*** See *The Tempest*, 5.1.50-57.

Page 76. *…onto the public stage of active witness.* See p. 4.

Page 76. *…going and doing likewise.* See Luke 10:37.

Page 77. "…a renunciation of every learned intermediate clause." *Concluding Unscientific Postscript*, 25, 26, 28.

Page 77. "…But the Secret sits in the middle and knows." Robert Frost, *Collected Poems, Prose, and Plays* (New York: Library of America, 1970), 329 ("The Secret Sits").

Page 77n. **The Hongs note that this book is Johann Arndt's *True Christianity.*** See *Eighteen Upbuilding Discourses*, 529.

Page 79. "…indeed, he does not know what he himself wants!" *Eighteen Upbuilding Discourses*, 344.

Page 79. *…to such a degree before the face of God.* See p. 64.

Page 79. …establishing an absolute relationship with the absolute. See *Fear and Trembling*, 56, 62, 70, 81, 93, 97, 98, 111, 113, 120.

Page 80. "…we protect ourselves by hiding behind big

books." *Kierkegaard's Journals and Notebooks* 11.2:322/XI[2] A 376 (1854).

Page 80. "…he does not know how to stay quietly in his room." *Pensées*, by Blaise Pascal, tr. A. J. Krailsheimer (New York: Penguin Classic), 67 (Pensée 136 (139)).

Page 80. "…a year in which to think about their inner lives." *Kierkegaard's Journals and Notebooks* 8:349/X[4] A 291 (1851).

Page 80. "…cannot replenish itself by God's visit." *Kierkegaard's Journals and Notebooks* 2:260/VII[1] A 14 (1846).

Page 82. "…as pure as my authorship is profound and unselfish." *Kierkegaard's Journals and Notebooks* 4:354/VIII[1] A 630 (1848).

Page 82. "…I [now] regard myself as a reader of the books, not as the author." *The Point of View*, 12.

Page 82. …to do the same with his published versions. See, e.g., *Upbuilding Discourses in Various Spirits*, 5; *For Self-Examination*, 3.

Page 82. …so as "to acquire a sort of surrogate." *Kierkegaard's Journals and Notebooks* 1:20/AA:12 (1935).

Page 83. "…it is required that one must know whereof one speaks." *Upbuilding Discourses in Various Spirits*, 126-27.

Page 84. "…the remedy usually lies in your own hands." *One Half of Robertson Davies*, by Robertson Davies (New York: Penguin, 1978), 51-52.

Page 84. …according to Pascal, "why prison is such a fearful punishment." *Pensées*, 68 (Pensée 136 (139).

Page 85. .... **Alas, what a change.**" *Kierkegaard's Journals and Notebooks* 4:102/VIII[1] A 40 (1847).

Page 85. "…**the association with God is unconditionally unsociable.**" *Without Authority*, 22.

Page 86. "…**becomes a very grave sickness if it is developed one-sidedly.**" *Either/Or* II, 246-47.

Page 86. …**for "how in the world would we acquire these mental states in our age."** *Kierkegaard's Journals and Papers* 4:299/X[3] A 79 (1850).

Page 87. "…. **Religiousness…is in fact about talking softly with oneself.**" *Kierkegaard's Journals and Notebooks* 4:74, 75/VII[1] A 205 (1846).

Page 87. …**have helped open up "whole new vistas".** See p. 43.

Page 91. …**(to the point of, as Maughan-Brown maintains, *belief in*).** See p. 36.

Page 92. …**his equally famous sentiment about *living life forward*.** See p. 14.

Page 92. …**the ethical silence that "prioritizes actions over words."** See *Ethical Silence*, 90-91.

Page 94. …***my partner or my companion.*** See, for example, *Box 66, Sumac Lane: A Lively Correspondence on Sin and Sanctity*, by Edna Hong (New York: Harper and Row, 1989), dedication.

Page 94. "…**for each to see the other whole and against a wide sky!**" *Rilke on Love and Other Difficulties*, tr. John J. L. Mood (New York: W.W. Norton & Company, 1975), 28.

Page 94. "…. I would go mad if I did housework all day." From Bo Elbrønd-Bek's "Kierkegaard in America: An Interview with Howard and Edna Hong" (Hong Kierkegaard Library Archives, no date).

Page 95. "…expected to devote themselves to their husbands' careers." "Love and Kierkegaard," by Marc Hequet in *Toward the Final Crossroads: A Festschrift for Edna & Howard Hong* (Macon, Georgia: Mercer University Press, 2009), 29.

Page 96. …silent absence akin to what George Steiner calls *real presence*. See *Real Presences*, by George Steiner (Chicago: University of Chicago Press, 1989).

Page 97. "…where the Word could get at me." *From This Good Ground*, by Edna Hong (Minneapolis: Augsburg Publishing House, 1974), 68, 73.

Page 98. "…but of something he had never had." *Bright Valley of Love*, by Edna Hong (Minneapolis: Augsburg Publishing House, 1976), 17, 18.

Page 98. "'…the tree that is your own Molly-self.'" *Box 66, Sumac Lane*, 89.

Page 98n. …how, that is, "the tree is to be known by its fruits." *Works of Love*, 14.

Page 99. …to begin "to exist in the truth one understands." See *Søren Kierkegaard's Journals and Papers* 2:537/IX A 438 (1848); cf. *Practice in Christianity*, 134.

Page 99. …(a concept to which Molly herself referred some 65 pages earlier). See *Box 66, Sumac Lane*, 25.

Page 99. "'…if you know only a smidge of that truth, you exist in that smidge.'" From an interview with the Hongs entitled "Facing Up to Age, Optimism Helps," by Kim Ode, *Minneapolis StarTribune*, November 3, 1998.

Page 99. ...to make manifest her most secret, wonderful, too big to grasp. See p. 00.

Page 100. "...the old familiar text handed down from the fathers." See p. 3.

Page 100. ...influenced by Kierkegaard: "Kierkegaard comes out in almost everything." "Kierkegaard in America: An Interview with Howard and Edna Hong."

Page 100. "...losing themselves in footnotes." *Søren Kierkegaard's Journals and Papers* 1:357/I A 146 (1836).

Page 102. "...chasing down the exact meaning of some word or phrase he used." Convocation address at St. Olaf College Boe Memorial Chapel by William Narum, December 3, 1976.

Page 102. ...so as not, in her words, to *go mad*. See p. 94.

Page 102. ...no use for "footnotes, cross-references, and all that scholarly paraphernalia." From "Literature as Handwriting on the Wall," by Edna Hong (Minnesota Humanities Commission lecture, Landmark Center, St. Paul, Minnesota, March 3, 1983), Hong Kierkegaard Library Archives.

Page 102. "...buttoning up points, for the sacrament of the altar." From "Leaving and Coming Home: Claiming the Sacrament at Home," by Edna Hong (College of St. Catherine Continuing Education and Summer Sessions; Theological Insights Programs: Walking in Two Worlds, Spring 1990; Hong Kierkegaard Library Archives.)

Page 103. "...to will the good is certainly difficult."

Concluding Unscientific Postscript, 354.

Page 103. "...he at once simply understands only the good." *Upbuilding Discourses in Various Spirits*, 25.

Page 103. *A fig tree, looking on a fig tree, becometh fruitful.* *Emerson's Essays and Lectures*, 58.

Page 104n. "...when one or all of them feels threatened." *The Gayety of Grace*, by Edna Hong (Minneapolis: Augsburg Publishing House, 1972), 17-19.

Page 105. "...and under the lampooning of men." *The Gayety of Grace*, 49-50.

Page 106. "...*You* did! You inserted the subject of women." *The Gayety of Grace*, 53-54.

Page 106. "...and nullify his principle of Grace!" *The Gayety of Grace*, 66.

Page 107n. "...which could exert equally powerful claims upon him." *Philosopher of the Heart*, xvii.

Page 108. ...a "rosebud" that "does not wither." From Kierkegaard's 1844 discourses entitled "Think about Your Creator in the Days of Your Youth" in *Eighteen Upbuilding Discourses*, 234, 241.

Page 109. "...you will never enter the kingdom of heaven." Matthew 18:3.

Page 109. ...in mature years "childhood transfigured." *Søren Kierkegaard's Journals and Papers* 1:117/II A 12 (1837).

Page 109. "...the Kingdom of the Second Spontaneity." *Clues to the Kingdom*, by Edna Hong (Minneapolis: Augsburg Publishing House, 1968).

Page 109. "...one that *believes* the text." See p. 36.

Page 110. "...which has the principle of and the power for ever-recurrent renewal." *From This Good Ground*, 76.

Page 110. "...systematic in-law relationship with the whole world." *Concluding Unscientific Postscript*, 5.

Page 111. "...plug all the ingresses of the soul." *From This Good Ground*, 67.

Page 111. "...and so he is built up." *Three Discourses on Imagined Occasions*, 62.

Page 112. "...be it good, bad, or indifferent." *From This Good Ground*, 33-34.

Page 112. "...even if you read the best of books." *Stages on Life's Way*, 364.

Page 113. "...and Pontoppidan's *Explanation of Luther's Small Catechism*." *Minneapolis StarTribune* April 5, 2007 Edna Hatlestad Hong obituary.

Page 113. "...any human being can pay" to a text. "Books in an Age of Post-Literacy," by George Steiner (*Publishers Weekly*, May 24, 1985), 46.

Page 113. "...and he essentially appropriates the essential by doing it." *Three Discourses on Imagined Occasions*, 38.

Page 114. "...merged and become one and the same." The Brothers Karamazov *and the Poetics of Memory*, by Diana Oenning Thomson (Cambridge: Cambridge University Press, 1991), 105.

Page 114. "...and I will tell you who you are." *Søren Kierkegaard's Journals and Papers* 1:121/X^2 A 97 (1849).

Page 115. "'...an openness to her that was like a full,

loving heart.'" *St. Paul Pioneer Press*, April 2007 Edna Hat-lestad Hong obituary, by Andy Rathbun.

Page 115. "...this wellspring from within was the essence of her being." *Toward the Final Crossroads*, 47.

Page 115n. ...conversations that existed outside the walls. See *Johannes Climacus*, 120.

Page 116. "...and translating is a creative sort of thing." "Kierkegaard in America: An Interview with Howard and Edna Hong."

Page 116. ".... And this she knew well." From "Times of Refreshing," a eulogy by Pamela Schwandt delivered at the memorial service for Edna at St. John's Lutheran Church in Northfield, Minnesota on Easter Saturday 2007. See *Toward the Final Crossroads*, 15, 16.

Page 117. "...the individual man and his mode of life." Søren Kierkegaard, *Edifying Discourses*, v. 3, tr. David and Lillian Swenson (Minneapolis: Augsburg Publishing House, 1945), x.

Page 117. ...what Viktor Frankl calls *tragic optimism*. See *Man's Search for Meaning*, by Viktor Frankl (Boston: Beacon Press, 1992), 139-40.

Page 120. "...filled with the boundless grace of God!" *The Gayety of Grace*, 51-52, 55-57.

Page 121. "...anyone preach about the seven deadly sins anymore." *Box 66, Sumac Lane*, 2, 26.

Page 121. ...was even possible in a human being. See p. 96.

Page 121. "...but continuing to serve it as long as possible." *Søren Kierkegaard's Journals and Papers* 6:447/X⁴ A

559 (1852). See also p. 72.

Page 122. "…to know when I have hurt someone I love." *From This Good Ground*, 73, 74.

Page 122. "…the "expression for the strongest self-assertion of existence." *Concluding Unscientific Postscript*, 528.

Page 122. "…my created-in-the-image-of-God birthright." *The Downward Ascent*, by Edna Hong (Minneapolis: Augsburg Publishing House, 1979), 13, 17.

Page 123. "…and thereby to establish him better in the good." *The Sickness unto Death*, 112.

Page 123n. In his translation of *The Sickness unto Death*…. *The Sickness unto Death*, tr. Bruce Kirmmse (New York: Norton, 2023), 146n5.

Page 123. "…your conduct in the relationships of your life." *Upbuilding Discourses in Various Spirits*, 137.

Page 124n. …by his pseudonym Vigilius Haufniensis in *The Concept of Anxiety*. *The Concept of Anxiety*, 16-24.

Page 124n. "…inwardness as the foundation for authentic speech and action." *Ethical Silence*, 18, 33, 65.

Page 125. "…provided us with solitude in good measure." Fr. "Remembering is a Forward Movement" by Edna and Howard Hong and Mary Hong Loe in *Growing Up in Minnesota: Ten Writers Remember Their Childhoods*, ed. Chester C. Anderson (Minneapolis: University of Minnesota Press, 1976), 229-30.

Page 126. "…to *all*, regardless of all human distinctions." "Leaving and Coming Home: Claiming the Sacrament at Home."

Page 127. "'…the crumbs from that table has not yet been woven.'" *The Hong Kierkegaard Library: A Crown Jewel of St. Olaf College*, by Jack Schwandt (Northfield, Minnesota: The Friends of the Kierkegaard Library, 2011), 24.

Page 128. "…she was being other-worldly in this world. She just was!" *Bright Valley of Love*, 134-35.

Page 128. "…to will to express in action precisely what he teaches." *Søren Kierkegaard's Journals and Papers* 1:265/VIII[1] A 554 (1848).

Page 128. "…and that "Christianity is the existential, a character-task." *Søren Kierkegaard's Journals and Papers* 1:773/III A 4 (1840) and 6:425/X[4] A 383 (1851).

Page 129. "…. Read him and let him speak for himself." *Box 66, Sumac Lane*, 25.

Works Cited

Anderson, Chester C., ed. *Growing Up in Minnesota: Ten Writers Remember Their Childhoods*. Minneapolis: University of Minnesota Press, 1976.

Barnett, Christopher P. *Kierkegaard, Pietism, and Holiness*. New York: Ashgate Publishing, 2011.

Bible, The. King James version.

Carlisle, Clare. *Philosopher of the Heart: The Restless Life of Søren Kierkegaard*. New York: Farrar, Straus and Giroux, 2019.

Davies, Robertson. *One Half of Robertson Davies*. New York: Penguin, 1978.

Dillard, Annie. *Pilgrim at Tinker Creek*. New York: HarperPerrenial, 1988.

Dostoevsky, Fyodor. *The Brothers Karamazov*. Translated by Richard Pevear and Larissa Volokhonsky. New York: Alfred A. Knopf, 1990.

Dylan, Bob. *"Love and Theft"* compact disc. New York: Columbia Records, 2001.

————. *Rough and Rowdy Ways* compact disc. New York: Columbia Records, 2020.

Elbrønd-Bek, Bo. "Kierkegaard in America: An Interview with Howard and Edna Hong." Hong Kierkegaard Library Archives, no date.

Emerson, Ralph Waldo. *Essays and Lectures*. New York: Library of America, 1981, 1983.

Evans, C. Stephen. *Kierkegaard and Spirituality*. Grand Rapids, MI: Eerdmans Publishing Company, 2019.

Frost, Robert. *Collected Poems, Prose, and Plays*. New York: The Library of America, 1995.

Geismar, Eduard. *Lectures on the Religious Thought of Søren Kierkegaard*. Minneapolis: Augsburg Publishing House, 1937.

Hay, Sergia. *Ethical Silence: Kierkegaard on Communication, Education, and Humility*. Lanham, Maryland: Lexington Books, 2020.

Hong, Edna H. *Clues to the Kingdom*. Minneapolis: Augsburg Publishing House, 1968.

——. *The Gayety of Grace*. Minneapolis: Augsburg Publishing House, 1972.

——. *From This Good Ground*. Minneapolis: Augsburg Publishing House, 1974.

——. *Bright Valley of Love*. Minneapolis: Augsburg Publishing House, 1976.

——. *The Downward Ascent*. Minneapolis: Augsburg Publishing House, 1979.

——. "Literature as Handwriting on the Wall." Minnesota Humanities Commission lecture, Landmark Center, St. Paul, Minnesota, March 3, 1983; Hong Kierkegaard Library Archives.

——. *Box 66, Sumac Lane: A Lively Correspondence on Sin and Sanctity*. New York: Harper and Row, 1989.

——. "Leaving and Coming Home: Claiming the Sacrament at Home." College of St. Catherine Continuing Education and Summer Sessions; Theological Insights Programs: Walking in Two Worlds, Spring 1990; Hong Kierkegaard Library Archives.

——. Edna Hatlestad Hong obituary. *Minneapolis StarTribune* April 5, 2007.

——. Edna Hatlestad Hong obituary, by Andy Rathbun. *St. Paul Pioneer Press* April 2007.

Hong, Howard V. and Edna H. Hong, editors. *The Essential Kierkegaard*. Princeton: Princeton University Press, 2000.

Kierkegaard, Søren. *Edifying Discourses,* v. 3, translated by David and Lillian Swenson. Minneapolis: Augsburg Publishing House, 1945.

———. *Fear and Trembling,* translated by Sylvia Walsh. Cambridge: Cambridge University Press, 2006).

———. *Kierkegaard's Journals and Notebooks,* 1-11. Edited and translated by Bruce Kirmmse et al. Princeton University Press, 2007-2020.

———. *Kierkegaard's Writings.* Howard V. Hong, general editor. Princeton; Princeton University Press, 1978-1998:

I. *Early Polemical Writings,* edited and translated with introduction and notes by Howard V. and Edna H. Hong, 1990.

II. *The Concept of Irony,* edited and translated with introduction and notes by Howard V. and Edna H. Hong, 1989.

III. *Either/Or* I, edited and translated with introduction and notes by Howard V. and Edna H. Hong, 1987.

IV. *Either/Or* II, edited and translated with introduction and notes by Howard V. and Edna H. Hong, 1987.

V. *Eighteen Upbuilding Discourses,* edited and translated with introduction and notes by Howard V. and Edna H. Hong, 1990.

VI. *Fear and Trembling* and *Repetition,* edited and translated with introduction and notes by Howard V. and Edna H. Hong, 1983.

VII. *Philosophical Fragments* and *Johannes Climacus,* edited and translated with introduction and notes by Howard V. and Edna H. Hong, 1985.

IX. *Prefaces* and *Writing Sampler,* edited and translated with introduction and notes by Todd W.

Nichol, 1997.

X. *Three Discourses on Imagined Occasions*, edited and translated with introduction and notes by Howard V. and Edna H. Hong, 1993.

XI. *Stages on Life's Way*, edited and translated with introduction and notes by Howard V. and Edna H. Hong, 1988.

XII. *Concluding Unscientific Postscript to* Philosophical Fragments, I, edited and translated with introduction and notes by Howard V. and Edna H. Hong, 1992.

XIV. *Two Ages*, edited and translated with introduction and notes by Howard V. and Edna H. Hong, 1978.

XV. *Upbuilding Discourses in Various Spirits*, edited and translated with introduction and notes by Howard V. and Edna H. Hong, 1993.

XVI. *Works of Love*, edited and translated with introduction and notes by Howard V. and Edna H. Hong, 1995.

XVII. *Christian Discourses* and *The Crisis and a Crisis in the Life of an Actress*, edited and translated with introduction and notes by Howard V. and Edna H. Hong, 1997.

XVIII. *Without Authority: The Lily in the Field and the Bird in the Air; Two Ethical-Religious Essays; Three Discourses at the Communion on Fridays; An Upbuilding Discourse; Two Discourses at the Communion on Fridays*, edited and translated with introduction and notes by Howard V. and Edna H. Hong, 1997.

XIX. *The Sickness unto Death*, edited and translated with introduction and notes by Howard V. and Edna H. Hong, 1980.

XX. *Practice in Christianity*, edited and translated with introduction and notes by Howard V. and Edna

H. Hong, 1991.

XXI. *For Self-Examination* and *Judge for Yourself!*, edited and translated with introduction and notes by Howard V. and Edna H. Hong, 1990.

XXII. *The Point of View: On My Work as an Author; The Point of View for My Work as an Author; Armed Neutrality*, edited and translated with introduction and notes by Howard V. and Edna H. Hong, 1998.

XXIII. *The Moment* and *Late Writings*, edited and translated with introduction and notes by Howard V. and Edna H. Hong, 1998.

XXV. *Kierkegaard: Letters and Documents*, translated with introduction and notes by Henrik Rosenmeier, 1978.

————. *Purity of Heart is to Will One Thing*, translated by Douglas Steere. New York: Harper and Row, 1948.

————. *The Sickness unto Death*, translated by Bruce Kirmmse. New York: Norton, 2023.

————. *Søren Kierkegaard's Journals and Papers*, 1-7. Edited and translated with notes by Howard V. and Edna H. Hong. Commentary by Gregor Malantschuk. Bloomington: Indiana University Press, 1967-1978.

Kirmmse, Bruce. *Kierkegaard in Golden Age Denmark*. Bloomington: Indiana University Press, 1990.

LeFevre, Perry D. *The Prayers of Kierkegaard*. Chicago: University of Chicago Press, 1956.

Lorentzen, Jamie. *Kierkegaard's Metaphors*. Macon, GA: Mercer University Press, 2001.

————, ed. *Toward the Final Crossroads: A Festschrift for Edna & Howard Hong*. Macon, GA: Mercer University Press, 2009.

———— and Marino, Gordon, eds. *Taking Kierkegaard*

Personally: First Person Responses. Macon, GA: Mercer University Press, 2020.

Malik, Habib C. *Receiving Søren Kierkegaard: The Early Impact and Transmission of His Thought*. Washington, D.C.: The Catholic University of America Press, 1997.

Maughan-Brown, Frances. *The Lily's Tongue: Figure and Authority in Kierkegaard's Lily Discourses*. Albany, NY: State University of New York Press, 2019.

Narum, William. Convocation address at St. Olaf College Boe Memorial Chapel. December 3, 1976.

Ode, Kim. "Facing Up to Age, Optimism Helps." *Minneapolis StarTribune*, November 3, 1998.

Pascal, Blaise. *Pensées*, translated by A. J. Krailsheimer. New York: Penguin Classic, 1995.

Pattison, George. *Religion and the Nineteenth-Century Crisis of Culture*. Cambridge: Cambridge University Press, 2009.

Rilke, Marie Ranier. *Rilke on Love and Other Difficulties*, translated by John J. L. Mood. New York: W.W. Norton & Company, 1975.

Schwandt, Jack. *The Hong Kierkegaard Library: A Crown Jewel of St. Olaf College*. Northfield, Minnesota: The Friends of the Kierkegaard Library, 2011.

Shakespeare, William. *The Riverside Shakespeare*. Boston: Houghton Mifflin Company, 1974.

Steiner, George. "Books in an Age of Post-Literacy," *Publishers Weekly*, May 24, 1985.

————. *Real Presences*. Chicago: University of Chicago Press, 1989.

Swenson, David. *Something About Kierkegaard*. Minneapolis: Augsburg Publishing House, 1941 and 1945.

Thomson, Diana Oenning. The Brothers Karamazov *and the Poetics of Memory*. Cambridge: Cambridge

University Press, 1991.

Thoreau, Henry David. *Walden*, ed. Walter Harding. New York: Houghton Mifflin Company, 1995.

Watkin, Julia. *Kierkegaard*. London: Continuum, 1997.

Wiman, Christian. *My Bright Abyss: Meditation of a Modern Believer*. New York: Farrar, Straus, and Giroux, 2013.

Acknowledgments

A thousand thanks to Andy Burgess for early discussions related to my manuscript, for his generous support in efforts to publish this and earlier manuscripts of mine, and also for his dear and longstanding friendship.

Many people closely read and made astute comments on early drafts of specific sections of this manuscript. Thank you Vivian Corres, Michael Daugherty, Kristen Eide-Tollefson, C. Stephen Evans, Donald Fox, Helen Gangsei, Elise Graber, Louise Griffin, Karen Hanson, Sergia Hay, Mary Hong Loe, Bruce Kirmmse, Karl Korbel, Ed Langerak, Cynthia Lund, Frances Maughan-Brown, Peter Narum, Matt and Monte Peterson, Marcia Robinson, Vanessa Rumble, George Slanger, Inger Stenseth, Anna Louise Strelis Söderquist, Ted Tollefson, and always, always, always my dear wife, Jane.

Index

Index

duplexity (see double-mindedness).
Dylan, Bob, 46, 75; *Rough and Rowdy Ways* CD, 137; *"Love and Theft"* CD, 141.
e——e, 19.
earnestness, 81.
Elbrønd-Bek, Bo, 94.
Eliot, T. S., 65.
Emerson, Ralph Waldo, 68-69.
Emerson: Essays and Lectures, 139, 146.
Erbauungsliteratur [edifying or upbuilding literature], 9.
Essential Kierkegaard (ed. Howard and Edna Hong), 139.
eternal, the, 17, 59, 63, 117; e. crashing into time, 38; "man's umbilical cord to the", 96, 121; e. happiness, 34, 77.
eternity, category of, 85.
ethical, the, 6, 44, 60, 124n; action, 102; communication, 54, 91; -religious, 6, 30, 44, 53; self-honesty, 45.
Ethical Silence: Kierkegaard on Communication, Education, and Humility (Sergia Hay), 89, 91, 124n, 143, 149.
Eucharist, 126.
Evans, C. Stephen, 31-32.
existence, 35, 128; etymology of, 76, 128.
existing religiously and humanly, 35-36, 128;

existing in the truth one understands, 61, 83, 99.
Explanation of Luther's Small Catechism (Erik Pontoppidan), 113.
faith, knight of, 79; as restless, 14.
feuilletons, 12.
footnote, 44, 100-02, 107.
Fox, Rev. Donald, 9.
Franke, August Hermann, 9.
Frankl, Viktor, 117.
Freemasonry, 48.
Frost, Robert, 77.
Geismar, Eduard, 33n, 64, 71, 78.
God, 11, 16, 19, 41, 44, 50, 60, 64, 71, 78-79, 85, 96-97, 106, 114, 117-19, 121, 123; conference with, 8; -consciousness, 117; G.'s visit, 80-81; grace of, 11, 51, 105, 118-20; hearing voice of, 74; as Hound of Heaven, 96; Kierkegaard as scribe in office of, 16; -man, 63; misery and, 11; needing, 11, 31, 33-35, 43, 63, 117, 119; -relationship, 85-86; recollection of the Word of, 40; as shy rabbit, 97.
Golden Age Denmark, 12-13.
good, the, 67, 103, 123; boring categories of, 68.
grace, 39, 52, 105-06, 108, 118-19, 124n, 129.
Grandmother Almina Egeland, 23, 25, 32-33, 47, 63, 89, 91.

Index

Index

Index

solitude (devotional), 84-85, 93-94, 124-25; see monasticism.
Something About Kierkegaard (David Swenson), 30, 134.
sorrow, 19, 73.
soul, 45, 110.
Spener, Philipp Jacob, 9.
spiritual trial, 1, 34-35, 37.
spontaneity (first; second), 109-10, 113.
Steere, Douglas, 64.
Steiner, George, 96.
Streams in the Desert (L. B. Cowman), 112.
striving borne of gratitude, 39.
suffering, 11, 68, 71, 73, 88, 108, 127, 129; joy in, 72-73.
"suspicious character" (self as), 72.
Swenson, David, 8, 30-32.
Swenson, Lillian and David, 117.
Taking Kierkegaard Personally (eds. Jamie Lorentzen and Gordon Marino), 46n, 66n, 136-37, 139-40.
Tauler, Johannes, 9, 10, 123n.
temporal, the, 45, 63.
Tersteegen, Gerhard, 9.
Thomas à Kempis, 9, 69, 123n.
Thompson, Diane Oenning, 114.
Thompson, Francis, 96.
Thoreau, Henry David, 29.
Thorvaldsen, Bertel, 52-53, 55-56.
time, 54, 59.

Toward the Final Crossroads: A Festschrift for Edna & Howard Hong (ed. Jamie Lorentzen), 144, 148.
Tolstoy, Leo, 48.
Toynbee, Philip, 96.
tragic optimism, 117.
transfiguration, 109, 123, 129.
True Christianity (Johann Arndt), 11, 78n.
umbilical cord to the eternal (see the eternal).
understanding life backward, living life forward, 14, 91-92.
Unitarianism, 48.
unsociability, 85, 91.
upbuilding (the; the edifying), 7-8, 10, 29, 44, 74, 78-79, 111.
upbuilding discourses, 36.
Valbracht, Rev. Louis, 49, 51, 56-60.
vocabulary (religious) (see the religious).
Walsh, Sylvia, 133.
War and Peace (Tolstoy), 48.
wars, 32.
Watkin, Julia, 30-32, 134.
wild bird, 72.
Wiman, Christian, 54.
witness (active), 12, 15, 40, 76, 129.
wonder (obedient), 36.
Word, the, 114, 121.
youth (see child).

169